MW01107897

MONTANA
HUNTING GUIDE

By Dale Burk

Published in the United States of America

MONTANA HUNTING GUIDE

Dale A. Burk

Copyright 1985 by Dale A. Burk

Library of Congress Catalog No. 83-60660

ISBN 0912299-16-9

Cover Photo
The montage of photographs on the front cover show a variety of Montana big game animals and hunting scenes. Thanks to Gary Holmes and Ed Wolff for their permission to use the Canada goose, mule deer and elk scenes. Other photos on the cover and throughout the book, unless otherwise credited, were taken by the author. The photo of the author on the back cover was taken by his brother, Stoney Burk.

Stoneydale Press Publishing Company
304 Main Street — Drawer B
Stevensville, Montana 59870
Phone:406-777-2729

Table of Contents

Dedication

To my friend, colleague and fellow hunter, Jack Atcheson Sr. — for all he has done over the years on behalf of hunters and the sport of hunting.

Introduction

From the outset, let me say that the doing of this book has been an undertaking of unabashed joy in the face of sometimes gruelling effort. I love hunting. And I enjoy sharing that experience, be it with a hunting partner in the field or through the process of writing about it. I also know that writing, like hunting, is best accomplished when you work through difficult odds to achieve a goal that may mean nothing to anyone but yourself. The completion of this book represents, to me, the cresting of a ridge I've wanted to top for a long, long time. I believe that Montana hunting is something special and it was important to me, in approaching a book such as this, to consider not only what it is that makes hunting in Montana extraordinary, but what it will take to keep it that way. I know that my father's generation did that for me, something the two previous generations had not done for his.

Hunting is, has been, and likely ever shall be, a part of my very being. It is as much a part of my life as is the home in which I live, the things I do to make a living, and the associations I cherish with numerous friends, family and loved ones. It is a part of my life I give much thought and consideration to because, fortunately, I *know* the fulfillment it provides me.

From my earliest days, if my recollections serve me properly, hunting has been a part of my life. I got my introduction to it at what some would call a tender age, the preschool years when I was taken on trips into the woods by my father and grandfather.

Then, at 12, I took my first whitetail buck with one shot from an old 25-35 Winchester 94 carbine; shortly after that a six-point bull elk fell to that same rifle. I was a hunter hooked for life, literally. Thus I came to hunting with an innocence of tradition. Only later would I realize that hunting was also an endeavor in which I personally had both philosophical and ethical questions to answer. If I was to enjoy the spoils of hunting — the time in the field, the taking of game and venison or elk meat for the table — I also had to give something back to it, to the future, to my children, as had been done for me.

It is my hope that this book qualifies, in some manner, as part of the payment of that debt. I also hope it expresses some of the joy — and even ecstacy — I've experienced hunting in Montana. But I also trust that within these pages I've given adequate recognition to the hundreds of individuals who have made Montana hunting, my hunting and yours, the joy it really is. Some of them, friends and professional associates alike, are listed by name in the text that follows. Many others are not and I trust that they will read themselves into the text; they know who they are and what they've accomplished.

No project like this is completed without the assistance of many, many people. I'd like to extend special thanks to some who provided help beyond the ordinary, however. These include my good friend and associate, Phil Tawney, who encouraged me to produce a thorough guide to hunting in Montana and who kept encouraging me in the face of month after month of laborious research and writing work; Ron Aasheim and Bill Phippen of the Montana Department of Fish, Wildlife and Parks, who provided liaison with that agency; Robin Tawney, for her meticulous editing of a rough text into a workable manuscript; and photographers Ed Wolff, Gary Holmes and Stoney Burk, for the cover photographs they provided.

Dale A. Burk
Stevensville, Montana
August 1985

Chapter One

A Look at Hunting in Montana

When Lewis and Clark's Corps of Discovery entered what is now Montana in late April of 1805, they immediately encountered multitudes of big game animals and excellent hunting. Elk, mule deer, buffalo and grizzly abounded and their designated hunter, John Drouillard, had no trouble providing the Corps' crew with the meat they needed to sustain their arduous upriver labors. That good fortune of plentiful game and good hunting adjacent to the Missouri River lasted until the party reached the river's headwaters in the mountainous terrain we now know as the Centennial Mountains. There and on into the Bitterroots, even Drouillard, who surely would be among any listing of the dozen or so best hunters ever to ply the endeavor in Montana, had trouble finding game.

In fact, the members of the exploring party became so desperate for meat that they killed and ate several of their horses. The literal glut of game in the broken prairie land east of the mountains was precisely opposite the shortage of big game animals in the Centennials and Bitterroots, a dilemma that stands in stark contrast to the situation today. One hundred and eighty years later even average hunters can find and take elk and deer regularly in either the Centennials or the Bitterroots and, while the buffalo and elk aren't to be found in much of the land along the Missouri in northcentral and eastern Montana, deer abound and hunting is outstanding by anybody's yardstick.

It is human nature to remember and embellish the good in our past and forget the bad; thus is born on the wings of faulty memory the notion of the "good old days." It is a tendency we can easily forgive, whatever the time frame in which we perceive the relationship. I hear it in Montana even today when comparing hunting in the 1980s with hunting 10, 20 or even 30 years ago. Always, the inference is that hunting was somehow better in those "good old days."

Well, that just ain't necessarily the case in regard to big game hunting in Montana. Certainly it isn't the case with deer, elk or antelope though obviously the glory days of hunting for buffalo and grizzly bear are over. Whitetail and mule deer hunting potential are at all-time highs in Montana in the 1980s. So is elk hunting, which has increased incredibly in the past three decades as elk have expanded their range into territory in northwestern and western Montana where they were seldom encountered 30 years ago.

And yet the myth persists that hunting was somehow better in bygone years, which it undoubtedly was if you evaluate it only in terms of many, many fewer hunters perhaps doing well but only taking a tiny percentage of the number of animals harvested today at greatly expanded and sustainable levels. The fact is that many more hunters go afield today and far more animals are taken each year than in the past. Things are a lot better than some would make them out to be and, in fact, we not only have many more people enjoying the sport of hunting today, our seasons are longer and our hunting variety has expanded.

Professional wildlife management people in Montana, frustrated at what they knew was a misconception of this relationship of present to past hunting opportunities, in 1980 issued a summary comparing hunting over a 30-year span in Montana — 1948 to 1980. Here are some of their major findings:

Deer

• In 1948 the general deer season ran from Oct. 15 to Nov. 15. Approximately one-third of the state in central, southwestern and northwestern Montana was open for bucks with antlers at least four inches long. More than one-third of eastern and northern Montana was closed to all deer hunting. About one-fourth of the central and southcentral part of the state had short deer seasons of either three or nine days. The only either-sex seasons were in a small area in the Big Hole Valley and in three small parts of the upper Madison Valley.

• In 1980 the general deer season ran from four to six weeks and the entire state was open to bucks of either species with antlers of four inches or longer. Much of western Montana had three- or eight-day either-sex hunting at the beginning of the season while a part of southcentral Montana had a week of either-sex hunting at the end. For much of northern and eastern Montana, the general season was for antlered buck mule deer and either-sex whitetailed deer. In addition, approximately 2,000 either-sex permits in southwestern Montana and nearly 6,000 B tags for specific age and/or sex of a second deer were available in much of central and eastern Montana.

Photo courtesy Montana Department Fish, Wildlife & Parks

Hunting in Montana was largely wide open until the late 1800s and plentiful game could be found throughout the state. Here a party of hunter-trappers display a take of elk, mule deer, bighorn sheep, mountain goat, coyote and other species. No date was available for the photograph.

Elk

• In 1948 the general elk season also ran from Oct. 15 to Nov. 15 and approximately one-fifth of western Montana was open for elk hunting. About half of the open areas was either-sex and the other half was divided between bull and branch-antlered bull bag limits. Elk seasons were complicated with 42 different, special seasons on the map in addition to the general season. Seasons were listed by county or portions of counties. Season dates were variable with some areas next to Yellowstone National Park in Park and Carbon counties opening as early as Sept. 15. Smaller portions of Beaverhead, Deer Lodge and Silver Bow counties opened as late as Dec. 31. Seasons closed as early as Oct. 31 in Ravalli County and as late as Feb. 28 in many areas.

• In 1980 more than half the state was open to elk hunting from Oct. 19 or Oct. 26 to Nov. 30 in most areas. While the general bag limit was antlered bulls, some portions of western Montana had a week of either-sex hunting at the beginning of the season; other either-sex seasons remained open until a quota had been reached. In addition, more than 5,000 antlerless or either-sex permits were issued. More than 4,000 permits were also available for late hunts at Gardiner and in the Gallatin Valley.

Antelope

• In 1948 all or portions of 23 counties were open for antelope hunting, less than half the area east of the Continental Divide. Season lengths ranged from 8 to 29 days. A total of 750 either-sex, doe-only and 1,825 buck-only permits were issued (2,675 total).

• In 1980 92 hunting units, essentially the entire state east of the Continental Divide, were open to antelope hunting. More than 16,000 either-sex permits were issued. With the exception of three hunting units, hunters had 29 days in which to hunt.

Bighorn Sheep

• There was no bighorn sheep season in 1948.

• In 1980 limited hunting was offered in 17 units and unlimited licenses were available in seven units. Eighteen "any" ram, 30 "legal" ram (3/4 curl or larger), 115 adult ewe, and 57 either-sex permits were issued in the limited areas (220 total) and a combined quota of 31 "legal" rams was established in the unlimited areas. Most hunting seasons ran from Sept. 15 to Nov. 30.

Moose

• In 1948 moose hunting was confined to eight areas in southwestern Montana and 80 mature bull permits were issued. The season in four small units bordering Yellowstone National Park in south Park County ran from Sept. 15 to Nov. 15, while the dates for the other four areas were Oct. 15 to Nov. 15.

• In 1980 moose hunting was allowed in 53 units covering most of western and southwestern Montana; 266 either-sex and 271 antlered bull permits were issued (537 total). The general season extended from Sept. 15 to Nov. 30 in western Montana and from Oct. 19 or Oct. 26 to Nov. 30 in southwestern Montana.

Bear

• Black bear hunting opportunities were similar in 1948 and 1980, one per hunter statewide with the season running from spring through the fall big game season. The grizzly season was also similar, coinciding with fall big game dates, except that in 1980 grizzly hunting was restricted to the "Bob Marshall Ecosystem" in northwestern Montana with a total man-caused mortality quota of 25.

• A major difference was that in 1948 only one black bear or grizzly could be taken, while in 1980 one of each could be taken.

Upland Birds

• In 1948 the upland bird seasons were much simpler, a 12-day statewide pheasant season and a five-day sharptailed grouse season in 16 eastern and northern counties (only two days for grouse in 13 central counties). The bag limit was three grouse and three cock pheasants daily and in possession. Shooting hours were from 8 a.m. to 5 p.m. The season was closed on sage grouse, blue grouse, ruffed grouse, Franklin's grouse and chukar and Hungarian partridge. The first transplant of wild turkeys was not to take place for another six years. In summary, 17 days

Photo courtesy Montana Department Fish, Wildlife & Parks
The once-plentiful buffalo were slaughtered by the thousands in Montana simply for their hides and the endless herds had disappeared by the 1870s.

of upland bird hunting opportunity existed and six birds daily and in possession were allowed.

• In 1980 seasons provided for 43 days of pheasant hunting, up to 93 days for Hungarian partridge and chukar partridge, and up to 86 days for sage grouse, sharptail grouse, blue grouse, ruffed grouse and Franklin's grouse. In addition, spring and fall seasons were conducted for wild turkey. Shooting hours were from one-half hour before sunrise to one-half hour after sunset. A hunter could have hunted 93 consecutive days for upland birds during 1980 and bagged as many as 22 birds per day (excluding turkey) with twice that many in possession.

Migratory Birds

• In 1948 the migratory bird season consisted of two 14-day periods, Oct. 8-21 and Nov. 12-25. The daily bag limit was five ducks and four geese (no more than two dark geese) and the possession limit was 10 ducks and four geese. The season was closed statewide on Ross' geese, whistling swans and little brown cranes, and the season was closed on white geese in Gallatin, Madison and Beaverhead counties. Shooting hours were from one-half hour before sunrise to one hour before sunset, except on opening day when the season opened at noon.

• In 1980 the migratory bird season was 93 days in the Pacific Flyway portion of the state and 83 days in the Central Flyway. Seven ducks per day could be bagged in the Pacific Flyway and as many as 10 per day under a point system in the Central Flyway, with twice as many allowed in

—13—

A carbine in the hands of a well-dressed young lady could provide a couple of nice mule deer bucks in early wildlife days in Montana. Deer have been the state's most widespread game animal throughout its history.

possession. Five geese per day and in possession were allowed in the Pacific Flyway (no more than two dark or three white, including Ross' geese), and two per day and four in possession were allowed in the Central Flyway. In addition, 500 whistling swan permits were issued for Teton County and a 37-day little brown crane season in central Montana carried a bag limit of three and a possession limit of six. Shooting hours ran from one-half hour before sunrise to sunset.

What does all this mean? Do we really have more game now? Is hunting actually better or are we experiencing higher harvest levels at the expense of the future? Gene Allen, who was administrator of the Montana Department of Fish, Wildlife and Parks' Wildlife Division in 1980 and who now is unit supervisor for field services, put the situation in perspective. "The real difference has been the arrival, development and success in Montana of a sound wildlife management program based on fact," he said. "Wildlife management has been defined as the art of making land produce sustained annual crops of wild game for recreational use. It recognizes that wildlife is a product of the land, that each year a 'biological surplus' exists, and that this surplus can removed by sport hunting without affecting the breeding stock or next year's population levels."

I found Allen's comments and the comparison of the 1948 situation to that of 1980 extremely interesting because my own involvement in hunting in Montana began in 1948. I was 12 then and took my first buck that fall, a whitetail, atop a high ridge to the northwest of Kalispell. I have

This 1914 photograph shows a party of hunters and their take along the Missouri River. They are identified as Sam Rugg, Jim Greenon, Harry Yotter, William Jaycox and Dr. Mark Hoyt.

hunted the state ever since and for some 20 years now have also been an observer and commentator on the practice and politics of wildlife management. I believe that, by and large, wildlife management has worked and worked well, but like most hunters I hadn't bothered to really think through the situation in terms of the vast changes that have taken place — not only in regard to increased hunting opportunities but also the incredible increases that have occurred in human population, land development, logging and roading, mineral exploration and development, and so on. To me it is a minor miracle that hunting has held its own, let alone gotten better and not worsened during the time period Allen outlined in his report, which incidentally he titled "How Good were the Good 'Ol Days?"

Allen insisted that wildlife management came of age in Montana in the 1950s, after really arriving as a practiced concept in the early 1940s. Since then it has attempted to keep pace with rapid and increasing demands on the resource base, with wildlife habitat being the most critical. It has come to a point that pressures against wildlife and the future of hunting in Montana threaten to erase achievements that have brought hunting to the levels it enjoys today.

"Successful wildlife management requires an understanding of animal ecology, or the relationship(s) between an animal and its environment," Allen said. "It requires a knowledge of animal distribution and movement patterns. It recognizes habitat as the single most important element — the element responsible for the year-to-year stability and health of wildlife

Photo courtesy Montana Department Fish, Wildlife & Parks

An early-day hunting camp near Boulder gives an idea not only of the kinds of game taken, but the sort of camp and transportation used by the hunters of a bygone era in Montana.

populations. Finally, wildlife management must integrate all of these with a knowledge of 'other' uses of the land and the desires of private landowners and put it all together into an understandable package acceptable to the sporting public."

All this, of course, has only historic relationship to the situation that Lewis and Clark found in 1805. Their task was to explore the country and record what they saw; to them the presence or lack of game meant survival. Little regard could have been expected or was given to the future of wildlife, and most likely their assumptions would have been similar to those that existed in this country long past the end of frontier days. Wildlife had always been there and always would be.

Montana's history, however, like that of other places with a rich wildlife heritage, proved otherwise. The depletion of wildlife resources began with the advent of the fur trappers, who arrived on the heels of the Lewis and Clark Expedition, heightened during the period of mineral discovery and exploitation, and continued unabated into this century. Both sport and subsistence hunting took their toll, but ultimately it would not be the hunter's gun that caused the most impact but the changes in land use practices, particularly the commitment of vast acreages to commercial agricultural uses. It was both natural and understandable that wildlife populations would decrease as the habitat that sustained them was converted to uses which conflicted with their needs.

As was usually the case, however, the advent of "civilization" to Montana brought with it an obvious and continual decline in game animals that provided not only sport but subsistence to many who grubbed a living out of a generally inhospitable environment. First went the buffalo, then the bighorn sheep and finally the elk in all but the mountainous terrain where they were relatively safe from man's intrusion. It wasn't these subsistence hunters who threatened wildlife populations in Montana, however. It was the commercial hide and fur hunters, who decimated the buffalo, deer, beaver, grizzly, wolf and other species for the market value of their hides. Later the meat or market hunters did the same with elk, only this deadly gambit took on a grisly twist. Elk by the thousands were slaughtered only for their canine "ivory" teeth, which were used in the East for jewelry.

The upshot of all this was that many people in Montana realized what was taking place and moved to do something about it. The first conservation law passed in Montana came in 1869 as the Territorial Legislature closed the hunting season on introduced game birds. As early as 1872 the annual hunting season was closed from Feb. 1 to Aug. 5 on buffalo, deer, bighorn sheep, moose, mountain goat, deer and hares. Market hunting for game birds was prohibited in 1877. Certainly these restrictions were little more than a slap on the hand compared to today's highly regulated hunting conditions, but they were a beginning. Montana became a state in 1889 and its first laws continued the protection of bison, quail, moose, elk and beaver. The open season on deer, mountain goat, mountain sheep and antelope was set for Sept. 15 through Dec. 31.

Even by 1895, the legislature had provided for the establishment of a Fish and Game Board. Its responsibilities included establishing quotas on big game animals and setting hunting seasons. The restrictions it set are indicative of the attitude prevalent at the time: No license was required and hunters could bag eight deer, eight bighorn sheep, eight mountain goats, eight antelope, two moose and two elk. What a good thing it was that the human population was only a fraction of what it is today and that transportation was limited to horse-drawn vehicles!

The key is that the foundation had been laid. Wildlife conservation was in the process of firmly establishing itself in the psyche of the Montana resident, hunter and nonhunter alike. The excellent book *Game Management in Montana* issued in 1971 by the Montana Fish and Game Department explained the situation perfectly: "While these first laws merely attempted to regulate hunting of game by proclamation, the measures enacted represented a sincere desire to protect and build up game populations. For the most part, the new laws were ignored by the settlers and not enforced by the Territory. However, when Montana became a state in 1889, the laws became more stringent and other management tools were added to the conservation program."

By 1905, it appeared that a handle had been gotten on things even though hunters were indignant that they had to buy their first resident Montana hunting license that year — at $1. Never mind that that "family

Photo courtesy Montana Department Fish, Wildlife & Parks.

Boat hunters in Montana's early days may not have used fancy inflated rafts, but their wooden boats served the purpose. The hunter in this undated photograph is shown with a mixed bag of whitetail buck, beaver and birds.

Sherman Williams of Stevensville poses with his Montana record typical mule deer buck, taken in the foothills east of Stevensville in 1973. It scored 204 3/8 Boone and Crockett points.

license" entitled the taking of three deer, one elk, and one antelope per season, and 10 grouse, prairie chickens, foolhens, pheasants, sage hens, partridges and turtle doves (mourning doves) per day during the establish- ed season.

What hunters then didn't realize was that a statement by the state's first State Game and Fish Warden, W. F. Scott, would prove prophetic. "The protection of game and fish should be self sustaining," Scott wrote in his biennial report to Governor Toole. "This can only be accomplished by those doing the hunting and fishing paying the cost of sport provided them. This, as a rule, would have the beneficial effect of keeping the public domain for the public, and make the task of buying or leasing large portions of public lands for private reserves more difficult. I am more than ever convinced that the general adoption of licenses for shooting game is the only means of insuring even a moderate supply of game in the future." He was right, of course. As writer-historian Vernon Craig of the Montana Department of Fish, Wildlife and Parks has noted, income from hunting and fishing license sales continues to pay most of the bill for fish and wildlife management to this day.

Even so, the wildlife history of Montana took a course similar to what had happened and would happen elsewhere in the face of a developing nation. The litany could have been anticipated: Season restriction after restriction was instituted for both birds and big game animals. Game

The member 2 Boone and
Crockett Bull # 419 4/8 #
Killed in 1958 by Fred
Mercer of Twin Bridges
Montana. Awarded Sage-
more Hill Medal in 1966.
There have been only 13 of
these medals awarded
since 1949.

Fred Mercer took this Montana elk in 1958 in the Ruby River country of southwestern Montana. A beautifully-symmetrical rack, it is Number Four on the all-time Boone and Crockett list, scoring 419 4/8 points. This photo by Duncan Gilchrist shows Mercer's elk at the annual convention of the Rocky Mountain Elk Foundation — which arranged to have the four top all-time elk heads on display.

preserves were established, the bighorn sheep season was closed in 1915; it would remain so until 1953. The last Audubon sheep was killed in Garfield County in 1916. The deer bag limit was reduced to one deer in 1917. Exotic species, particularly birds, were released in the state. A statewide buck law established in 1936.

But what of the years from 1936 on to the comparison date of 1948 mentioned by wildlife manager Allen? The basic answer, realizing that it's impossible to totally generalize the situation, was one of decline. Sure, efforts continued to "get at" the situation, but because most of the attemp-

Photo courtesy Steve Copenhaver

Sam Weiss of Lebanon, Pa., took this six-point bull elk in Montana's Scapegoat Wilderness while on an outfitted hunt with Copenhaver Outfitters. This has become one of the most widely publicized of elk photos taken in Montana because of the magnificence of the trophy.

ted solutions didn't address the real underlying problem of habitat destruction or diminishment, no real solutions came. Examples of well-intentioned, but ultimately failing, efforts were winter feeding programs, restocking programs, predator control efforts and buck-only laws. Also central to the doomed wildlife management programs of the era was the notion that the major drain on wildlife populations was the hunters' gun. In fact, just the opposite was true but it wouldn't be until 1941 when an event of watershed significance occurred in regard to wildlife management, and ultimately hunting, in Montana that things would be turned around. Gene Allen referred to it when he mentioned that the good hunting of today is largely the result of the advent of professional, biologically-based game management principles in the 1940s.

The milestone event was the passage in 1941 of an act in the Montana Legislature implementing in the state the Federal Aid in Wildlife Resoration Act passed by the U.S. Congress in 1937. That act, popularly known as the Pittman-Robertson Act, earmarked funds from a special excise tax on sporting arms and ammunition for wildlife management in the states. Thus, sportsmen would pay the way towards professional wildlife management, and the rewards that Allen outlined stem directly from that beginning in 1941.

For example, several things occurred with passage of that 1941 act that have helped bring about better hunting in Montana. One was a law prohibiting diversion of hunting license fees for purposes other than wildlife restoration. Another was that jurisdiction for setting all hunting seasons and regulations was transferred from the legislature to the Fish and Game Commission. The law also, for the first time, provided the authority and funds to hire a staff of trained game biologists to undertake sorely-needed programs of surveying game populations and to search for answers to the state's overwhelming wildlife populations.

"Recognizing this and its changing role in the administration of the State's wildlife resources, the Fish and Game Commission adopted scientific management of wildlife as a basic policy in 1941," Thomas W. Mussehl and F.W. Howell wrote in the book *Game Management in Montana.* "This policy called for a program of investigational work and a foundation of facts about game animals and their relationships to the environment as a basis for management...The Fish and Game Department, which previously served mainly to enforce legislative game policies, took on a new look."

New look, indeed! But in the wake of that change would ride diehard opponents to such change, opponents that even today would abandon scientific game management principles on the whim of the moment, the pursuit of private gain, or the shortsighted approach of those who even today think they can ignore biological reality. The not-so-sound practices of the past that almost led to the ruination of Montana wildlife, and thereby hunting, still haunt us. Each year we still hear the ghosts of the discredited past urging us to abandon sound biological principles, to winter-feed game, to ignore the protection of critical wildlife habitat, to abandon the hunting of females of the species even after it has been proven it must be done in some places to keep total game populations in balance with the habitat, and so on, ad infinitum.

It is both an old and a new story, one each of us has a share in writing. And living. The fact is that Gene Allen was right. There are some things about the good old days that weren't very good at all, and there are some things about that good present days that are simply outstanding. Big game hunting in Montana is one of the latter.

Chapter Two

This Place Called Montana

What is this place Montana that it is considered by many big game hunters to be among the very best hunting spots in the world? And what makes it different from other famous hunting areas?

Well, for one thing Montana is big even though its size pales when compared with that of Alaska. However, only a small percentage of Montana is placed off limits to hunting — basically seven Indian reservations, one national park and part of another — so the size factor is an important one. For another, its geography is so diverse that it offers incredible wildlife habitat variation and hunting opportunities. It contains vast tracts of undeveloped land, a situation ideal not only for quality wildlife habitat but quality sport hunting as well. It offers more diversity of huntable big game species than any other western state. The implementation of modern, scientific game management principles over the past four decades is paying huge dividends in terms of expanded and continuing hunting opportunities. Montana's hunting country is generally accessible throughout the hunting season to resident and nonresident alike. Unlike Alaska or Africa or other great hunting spots of the world, you can reach Montana on your own by vehicle from anywhere in the continental United States. Finally, Montana, most often, can be hunted without the necessity of gearing up for long sieges of extreme cold, extremely hot or extremely wet weather situations.

That's not to say that you won't encounter these kind of conditions in Montana. You can and perhaps will. It's simply that they're not a constant part of the hunting experience and seldom do they persist to ruin an entire

Fantastic wilderness hunting country, the South Fork of the Flathead River in the legendary Bob Marshall Wilderness. This September scene is common in the early season before snow comes to the Montana backcountry.

hunting trip. I do recall, however, one hunt several years ago in the upper Bitterroot Mountains with Lynn Smith, a friend from Texas, when he stepped off the plane in **mid-November** to 76 degrees Fahrenheit temperatures. For a week we encountered temperatures into the high 80s and hunting was at a virtual standstill as the game holed up and field conditions were almost unbearable. I've also seen week-long fall rains in the northwestern part of the state, particularly the South Fork of the Flathead and the North Fork country. Sometime during hunting season you also can expect a surge of arctic air to hit the state, causing temperatures to plummet to and hold at near-zero or even lower. Now these conditions don't make hunting impossible, but they can make it difficult and unpleasant. Keep in mind that they're the exception rather than the rule.

The notion that Montana holds a special place in the hunter's heart isn't new. In fact, that idea first set down in the writings of Meriwether Lewis shortly after he'd crossed the 104th meridian in April of 1805 and entered "truly a desert barren country" (what is now eastern Montana). Lewis wrote of that experience: "The whol face of the country was covered with herds of Buffaloe, Elk and Antelopes; deer are also abundant, but keep themselves more concealed in the woodland. the buffaloe, Elk and Antelope are so gentle that we pass near them while feeding, without apearing to excite any alarm among them; and when we attract their attention, they frequently approach us more nearly to discover what we are, and in some instances pursue us considerable distance apparently with that view".

—24—

The whole face of the country isn't "covered" with herds of game anymore, buffalo, deer or anything else. But it still produces sizable populations of 10 big game species in excess of the land's ability to sustain them; thus, hunting remains a major component of resource utilization and control of wildlife populations. Jack Atcheson Sr. of Butte, Montana, who for 30 years has conducted a worldwide consulting and booking agency for hunters, is unabashed in his assessment of Montana's big game hunting. "Montana is a hunter's paradise," he says. "Nowhere, including Alaska, has more native big game animals to hunt."

Those species are elk, bighorn sheep, mule deer, whitetail deer, Shiras moose, antelope, mountain goat, grizzly bear, black bear and mountain lion. Now there may once again be buffalo on the list, too. A law passed in 1985 provided authority to the MDFW&P to conduct carefully regulated hunts for buffalo that spill out of Yellowstone Park's excessive herd into the surrounding countryside. In addition there are numerous game birds like pheasant, several species of grouse, quail, partridge, turkey, and a variety of waterfowl species including the prized Canada goose and several species of ducks.

The temptation when thinking about hunting in Montana is to consider only the statistics, impressive as they are. However, it would be a mistake to overlook the drama of hunting in so vast and diverse a land. Not only is

In southeastern Montana, very dense timber often typifies the ridges and hillsides while the creek bottoms are marked by open meadows frequented by both elk and deer.

there a sense of challenge in terms of pitting your skill against the wiles of a wild animal on its home turf, but in many situations the hunter must deal with the capricousness of the weather, difficult terrain and other limitations. Ultimately, the hunter realizes that the true meaning of hunting comes from within himself or herself and is held in direct relationship to all the factors involved.

How popular is hunting in Montana? One yardstick might be the speed with which the state's legal limit of 17,000 nonresident licenses sell out. The $300 tag sold out in six days in 1985; in 1984 it took 19 days for all 17,000 of these licenses to be purchased. Hunting is obviously a seller's market in Montana, a point that Jim Herman, chief of the licensing bureau, noted in commenting on the unprecedented six-day sell-out of the nonresident permits. "This only reaffirms the growing interest out-of-state sportsmen exhibit for partaking in the outstanding hunting Montana offers," Herman said.

For the record, over 2.5 million days of hunting-oriented recreation occur annually in Montana — a figure that is sure to climb in the next decade. People who hunt contribute mightily to both the economy and the way of life in Montana, a situation that has been in existence here from the first aboriginal hunters to the present.

There are 147,138 square miles in Montana, which makes it a geographic region as large as the entire nation of Japan. It ranks fourth in size among the states and is approximately 550 miles across on its east-west axis. From north to south, Montana measures approximately 325 miles.

The state is divided in three general physiographic regions which roughly break down into fairly equal sections — the west, central and eastern. These sections are referred to physiographically as the Montane, the Piedmont, and the Midland. The reader is cautioned, however, to remember that these designations are made on the basis of geography and cannot be precisely indicated by drawing lines on a map.

The eastern third of the state falls in the Midland, which basically is an extension of the interior continental plains. This region is characterized by broad fertile valleys paralleled by back-stepped benches and bluffs. Changes in soil, climate and vegetation are more gradual in this area, which also is generally more arid than other parts of the state. Dry and wide open would be characterizing words for this region.

The central part of the state — from the foothills east of the Continental Divide to the beginning of the Midland — is a broad Piedmont zone of slopes beginning at 3,500 feet elevation and extending downward to portions of the Missouri River in northeastern Montana at 1,900 feet. Abrupt changes in soils are related to these changes in elevation. The isolated, lesser mountain ranges in Montana are within the Piedmont. Diverse landscapes and faily constant winds characterize this part of Montana.

The Montane region of western Montana is comprised of mountains,

Photo by Frank R. Martin

The common black bear, which also can be brown or cinnamon or a mixture of colors, is found throughout most of Montana and has become a fairly popular game animal — though most of those taken are bagged by hunters who just happen upon the critters.

which generally lie in a northwesterly direction as a series of 25 or more high, parallel ranges. This region is generally forested with many basins and valleys, some of which are marked by large rivers and broad bottomlands where most of the land is privately owned. The highest elevation exceeds 12,000 feet and the lowest 1,780. Elevation, climate, vegetation and soils change abruptly over short distances in the Montane. Forested, steep mountainsides and clear creeks and rivers characterize the region.

Approximately 92 percent of the land used in Montana generally falls into the categories of farming, ranching, grazing, timber, watershed management and recreation. The remaining 8 percent includes wasteland, rivers, streams, lakes and reservoirs, highways and roads, and urban areas.

Agriculture is the leading land use and economic activity in Montana. Beef cattle and wheat comprise the bulk of agricultural activity. Mining and manufacturing are the next two most significant economic activities, followed by outdoor recreation.

Montana is famous for its weather, notably the daily listings of some of its locales for the national low temperature on many winter days. What these figures don't show, however, is Montana's generally dry climate with very little humidity. The average annual precipitation in the state is approximately 15 inches with 18 inches falling in the mountainous western region and about 13 inches falling on the eastern prairie.

During the early hunting season, the weather is generally mild, although winter storms can and do move into the state at any time. Many years, however, see little or no snowfall even in the mountains until late October or early November. In November, the hunter usually can expect to encounter snow throughout the state and lots of it in the high mountains.

Of particular concern to the hunter is accessibility to both public and privately-owned land. Statistics show that about half of Montana's hunting takes place on private land and generally access is good and relationships okay. However, problems of access do exist (See Chapter 11) both in regard to some private land and areas of the public domain where land is either leased for commercial use or blocked by private land in front of it. For example, in one blatant case on the Bitterroot National Forest a private landowner in the area posted "No Trespassing" signs on roads and lands that weren't even his — it was public land. When rangers on the Bitterroot Forest were asked to check the situation they couldn't be bothered to go out and defend the public's interest. All it would have taken is for the Forest Service to simply remove the signs, but agency instead got on its high horse. The agency's warped sense of public responsibility was later defended at a public meeting by a Bitterroot Forest wildlife biologist who took offense to the notion that the Forest Service was either indifferent to or incompetent in regard to handling such obvious cases of defending the public's right of access to public land.

Whatever, you should still check with the land agency involved in a region when questions of access to public land arise. Most often the rangers and other field personnel are extremely helpful and most are, like you, hunters, so they sympathize with the need to insure public access to national forest and other public domain lands.

In eastern Montana, a vast majority of the land is privately owned and intermingled with Bureau of Land Management (public domain) lands, while in the western part of the state national forest lands dominate and access generally is better and easier. Issues of public access to public land are vital to the future of hunting in Montana because the the U.S. Forest Service manages almost 17 million acres in Montana and the Bureau of Land Management about 8 million. Other lands of significance to the sportsman includes about a half-million acres of national wildlife refuges spotted around the state (see Appendix A for listing), where hunting is permitted, and 1.1 million acres of national parks closed to hunting and seven Indian reservations totaling 8.3 million acres that are closed to all big game hunting by nontribal members.

At the same time, sportsmen mustn't lose sight of the need to promote good sportsman-landowner relations because a vast majority of Montana's land is privately owned. The state wildlife agency's Ron Marcoux estimates that at least 50 percent and possibly as much as 65 percent of hunting in Montana takes place on private land. "The future of hunting in Montana depends on the access we're able to maintain to these private lands," Marcoux said as he pointed out that most of that land is open to hunting.

Some land, however, is closed. In 1985 the Montana Legislature passed a law to help landowners who close part of their land, to communicate directly and more clearly with hunters and fishermen. A landowner now can deny entry to his or her land either by posting a written notice on the property's boundary (that provision of the law is the same as before) **or** by painting a post, structure or some other object with at least 50 square inches of fluorescent orange paint. In the case of a metal fence post, the entire post must be painted.

Erv Kent, administrator of the MDFW&P's Law Enforcement Division, said the notice must be placed at each outer gate on the property, at all normal points of access to the property and wherever a stream crosses an outer property boundary line, as stated in the law.

With a population of 800,000-plus, Montana is sparsely populated in comparison to most states — a factor that takes some getting used to

In much of northwestern Montana, the very heavily-timbered slopes with small openings like these at the head of a basin are excellent places to locate bull elk.

when it comes to picking up supplies while on a hunting trip. Resident and nonresident hunters alike learn to "gear up" early for gas and groceries as many service stations and convenience stores in the state's smaller towns close early — meaning, in some cases, 5 or 6 p.m. It can come as a real shock to drive 30 or 40 miles into a small town to get gas and groceries only to find everything closed up tight.

If that happens, and it very well might, remember that things aren't all that bad. That sparse human population in the midst of an expanse of varied mountain, prairie and badland terrain helps to provide the habitat base for the animals you're after. You might, occasionally, have trouble getting gas or groceries — but you do have good hunting opportunities. So, even if the adage doesn't directly apply, you can rest assured that while you can't have everything, hunting in Montana can be pretty good whatever other problems you encounter. Although it may be hard to remember, when it's dark and snowing and you're down to an eighth of a tank of gas and nothing's open, that you're smack dab in the middle of a hunter's paradise wherever you are in Montana.

Photo by Ed Wolff

Carefully regulated mountain lion seasons have provided excellent sport and trophy hunts in Montana. The lion is found throughout most of the state's timbered terrain and has come back from troubled times in the late 1960s and early 1970s.

Chapter 3

Elk

The mule deer may be the most commonly taken big game animal in Montana, but it isn't the most prized. That cherished status belongs to the elk *(Cervus elaphus)* — also known as the wapiti. The elk is unquestionably the premiere big game animal in Montana.

At the risk of expressing a deep-seated bias, let it be known that I believe that lofty status is fully justified. The elk is not only the most magnificent of trophies, but it offers the most palatable meat of all the animals hunted in Montana. In combination, it provides the perfect object of the hunter's quest. Elk are handsome. They're big and yet wary. They are smart, a true challenge to the hunter who practices the ethic of fair chase hunting. And they're sufficiently rare to make getting them a real accomplishment.

Be it known that I also firmly believe that when God decided to make the most graceful and beautiful of four-legged animals, the outcome was the elk — and in particular that version of it found in this part of the world, the Rocky Mountain or Yellowstone elk. He couldn't have created an animal more likely to fill us with awe and admiration and, at the same time, fulfill that aspect of our being that makes us hunters. No big game animal stirs the soul nor fulfills the intent and purpose of hunting more than the elk. It is the best of all that is good in Montana big game hunting.

The elk thrives in the mountainous western third of the state and is also found in isolated pockets elsewhere — a sizable herd lives along the Missouri River in northcentral Montana, another in the Little Belt Mountains and a smaller herd in the Sweetgrass Hills in Toole County.

Early elk hunters took what they wanted. No date is provided for this historic photograph of three hunters with seven elk, but obviously was taken in summer while the velvet was still on the antlers.

In the November-December 1984 issue of its magazine *Montana Outdoors,* the Montana Department of Fish, Wildlife and Parks listed the elk's status as "stable in most of western Montana and limited areas of eastern Montana." That was a comforting assessment to those of us who have fought bitterly over the past 20 years to preserve and, where possible, enhance the habitat elk need to remain a major component of the Montana hunting scene. Excessive roading into formerly wild areas, mining and mineral exploration, oil and gas leasing, subdivisions in key elk winter range, and generally increased human activity in areas vital for elk survival have threatened the stability of Montana's elk herds at different times and at varying degrees of severity for the last several decades. Now it appears that some of the efforts to preserve key elk habitat are paying off.

For many decades now, elk have been on a comeback trail in Montana and, while we can rejoice that great strides in their recovery have been made, sober judgment tells us that elk will never be restored to their original widespread range in Montana. Thus it becomes all the more critical to enhance the remaining vestiges of wildland habitat now providing that moderately-expanding population of elk.

For most of the century following Lewis and Clark's observance of abundant elk herds along most of their travel routes through Montana, elk were found almost everywhere with the possible exception of the heavy forests in the northwestern corner of the state. The mountainous terrain that now harbors elk did then, too, particularly in the foothills, while out on the Great Plains elk were common along the river breaks and wooded stream bottoms.

Settlement changed all that. Elk were virtually wiped out in eastern Montana and many other parts of the state where conflicts with humans always resulted in the elk being decimated. Thus, only fragment populations in the forested sections of the state remained of the once great herds. By the advent of the 1900s, only those remnant populations in the mountainous country and the large herds in and around Yellowstone Park and along the Continental Divide in northwestern Montana remained.

As has usually been the case in such matters, it was the hunter who both sought and achieved the restoration of Montana's elk herd — first through a restrictive hunting season (beginning as early as 1913) and a vigorous transplant program that was begun in 1910 and which still is putting elk into portions of the state that will support them.

More important in recent years, however, have been the aforementioned victories in terms of protecting critical elk habitat — through the acquisition of key winter game ranges, the closure of many logging roads in areas where elk needed the security of cover to survive, particularly on calving areas, and general recognition that elk herds that are both sizable and healthy don't come about by accident. An aggressive publicity campaign in the 1970s by sportsman's groups, most notably the Montana Wildlife Federation under Don Aldrich's leadership, the Montana Wilderness Association and the Montana Department of Fish, Wildlife and Parks, raised public awareness about what was needed to achieve quality elk management.

So did an incredible upswing in public interest in elk hunting, both in Montana and nationally. By and large it is the magic of elk and elk hunting that attracts nonresident hunters to Montana and, in combination with their fellow hunters in Montana, they make a fairly powerful lobby on behalf of elk and quality elk management. Not only do the fees those hunters pay for the privilege of hunting elk help in the cause of professional management, the existence of a built-in interest group helps give elk the status and political clout needed to preserve the wild land essential to elk.

If there's any doubt about either the mood of the elk hunter or the general interest in elk and elk hunting, one need only consider the phenomenon of a new and extremely influential national "elk interest group" organized over the past couple of years from a home base in Troy, Montana. Two years ago three northwestern Montana individuals who cared very much about elk — brothers Bob and Bill Munson of Troy and Charlie Decker of Libby — launched the Rocky Mountain Elk Foundation to promote not only the cause of sound, scientific elk management but the future of elk hunting. The Foundation has enjoyed incredible public acceptance and growth; today it publishes a fine, full-color magazine and its full-time staff is involved in promoting elk research, information

Terry Krogstad of Kalispell took this magnificent bull elk with the bow and arrow in the Flathead Valley. The prize trophy scored 356 and 7/8 points and resulted from a physically gruelling pursuit of the animal over several hours.

dissemination and management programs throughout the western states and Canadian provinces where elk are found, including Montana. (For a listing of the Foundation's address, see Appendix D.)

What is there about elk that it attracts such attention? A member of the deer family, the elk sports a coat of light brown with the head, neck and legs being darker than the rest of the body. It has a bright, distinctive rump patch that is yellowish to yellowish-orange. The mane or ruff is generally a dark brown to almost black-brown color; it is heavier and longer on bulls.

Photo by Neal Mischler

A bugling bull elk is shown with a portion of his harem. This fairly young bull has a smallish set of antlers.

Cows do not have antlers. The antlers of a mature bull usually have five tines projecting from the main branch for a total of six points. These antlers, in combination with the colorful combination of yellows and dark, rich browns of its mane, legs and underbelly provide the bull elk with a grace and sense of power and dignity enjoyed by few animal species.

Size is a constant source of argument among elk hunters because elk generally don't carry as much weight as a domestic cow or horse of the same height. A cow elk can weigh anywhere from 400 to 600 pounds while bulls generally weigh between 600 and 900 pounds, though some top 1,000 pounds. Whatever, elk are big — standing five feet or more at the shoulders — and many are the reports of hunters mistaking them for horses in brushy, timbered country or even occasionally in the open grasslands.

Elk are a species with a strong herd instinct and are generally defined in terms of the "herd" in which they happen to live — the Yellowstone, Flathead, Missouri, Little Belts, and so on. In fact, however, these herds are made up of single bulls and countless bands of three, five or seven elk of mixed sexes that are scattered throughout the forest environment and come together only at the mating season or in the winter months when weather requires them to concentrate on the lowland winter range. It isn't uncommon, however, to find as many as 20 or 30 elk in a band, particularly in terrain characterized by many open, grassy parks.

One characteristic worth noting is that each of these "bands" or small "herds" is generally controlled by an older cow — called a "lead cow" in the hunting fraternity. Often you can get right into the midst of one of these bands if the lead cow doesn't sense your presence there, but once she does, you can expect the elk to depart immediately. It's worth trying to work your way into a band of elk sometime if for no other reason than to learn their habits and methods of communication. The cows and calves make a soft, mewing sound when communicating with each other — and the cry of alarm, termed an elk's "bark" is a sharp, dog-like, distinctive sound any hunter who goes after elk regularly will hear more than once. Elk are not the easiest animal in the world to get close to.

No sound in the wild, however, comes close to matching the thrill of hearing the spine-tingling pitch of bull elk bugling in mating season, usually from mid-September to early Octobert. It is a sound of extreme importance to the early-season elk hunter. Numerous artificial "elk calls" are designed to imitate the elk's bugle and "bugling" has become extremely popular in recent years, particularly among bowhunters, as a means of calling elk into shooting range.

As recent as a decade ago, homemade calls were the vogue; most calls were made from either a section of twisted,"curley-cue," brass pipe or a short piece of plastic pipe with a whistle mouthpiece. Then came the development of a mouth diaphragm (actually an adaptation of diaphragms used elsewhere in the country for calling turkeys) and other more sophisticated reed calls that enabled closer imitation of the real elk bugle. Today there are a number of excellent calls on the market.

There are also numerous cassette lesson tapes, seminars, video programs and other aids to picking up knowledge about how to bugle elk, but in mentioning them, I'm reminded of a statement made by Rob

Hazlewood of Helena, who is a founder of the Cedar Hill Game Call Co., made at a seminar on bugling held in Great Falls a year ago. (Cedar Hill makes one of the most popular mouth diaphragm calls.) "Nothing can improve on actual practice in the woods, under field conditions, with your heart beating and your emotions doing all kinds of weird things," Hazlewood said. "You've got to combine whatever knowledge of calling you pick up with skill development in the field so that you'll learn how to react to a bull when he answers you."

The same holds true for elk hunting in the regular season. It pays to learn all you can about elk, their habits and their habitat. Now that isn't all that easy, given the incredible variation in habitat in which elk are found in Montana. From the arid, semi-desert country of the Missouri Breaks to the dense, boggy and extremely moist environment of the northwestern part of the state on to the dense lodgepole pine forests throughout much of the timbered mountain country or the open, grassy park-like settings of the southwestern and southern part of the state, elk prove nothing so much as that they can thrive in a variety of environments.

Whatever, some habits and characteristics are universal. One is their need for and love of wild land, their essential "security blanket" if you will. So vital is it to most elk that they'll travel long distances to get to it if disturbed or moved from one safe haven and required to flee to another. "If elk can depend on our society to preserve their natural environment, then we can depend on elk to remain a part of our wild lands," wrote John Cada, a game biologist with the Montana Department of Fish, Wildlife and Parks and one of the most knowledgeable elk researchers in the country, in an article in *Montana Outdoors.* So, look for wild land — remote basins, isolated drainages, ridges and stands of timber that are uncut and unroaded, generally inaccessible country — if you want to locate elk.

Next, look for water. Elk prefer being in a moist environment, whether it's wading and frolicking in the Missouri River in the harshly dry environment of the breaks or wallowing in a bog seep at the head of a high country basin in the snow-covered Bitterroots. Look, too, for combinations of water and dense timber, particularly in late summer or early fall; elk will stay in these damp, cool jungles so long as daytime temperatures remain high.

Like most members of the deer family, the elk's feeding activity is most often accomplished early in the morning or in the evening, though they often feed at night. Daytime hours generally find them secreted in a stand of lodgepole pine or along the crest of a timbered ridge where they have a good view of the surrounding countryside and lay down to chew their cud.

Elk are extremely adaptable when it comes to food, though they prefer native bunch grasses, particularly for winter food. Merle Rognrud and Reuel Janson, writing in the book *Game Management in Montana,* described the elk's feeding habits thus:

"Elk prefer native bunch grasses for winter food. However they are very adaptable and will feed on other grasses, sedges, forbs and browse. They also quickly acquire a taste for hay from ranchers' stacks. Elk feed heavily on green grass in the spring, but switch mostly to forbs such as dandelion, geranium, and aster in the summer. Grasses again become the most important food in the fall. On browse ranges, 90 percent of the winter diet and 50 percent of the summer diet may be browse. Their habitats are classified as browse ranges and grass ranges on the basis of winter food availability. Browse ranges predominate in the heavily forested areas of western Montana. There is general transition in plant composition from western browse ranges to east slope grass ranges. Major forage plants on browse winter ranges are willow, Ceanothus, maple, serviceberry, chokecherry, and sedges. These plants occur in greatest quantity on burned-over areas, where the forest canopy is absent or sparse. Elk populations thrive best during the shrub stages of plant succession. Elk numbers decline as coniferous trees invade the old burns and replace browse and herbaceous plants. Major forage plants on grass ranges are Idaho fescue, bluebunch wheatgrass and rough fescue".

A look at the statistical aspect of elk hunting in Montana reveals a rather startling fact: in spite of astronomical increases in the number of hunters afield, the kill over the past 40 years has remained quite constant. Generally the harvest has ranged from 11,000 to 14,000 with low takes of 6,400 in 1952, 7,657 in 1965 and 7,860 in 1976, and high kills of 16,700 in 1968 and 17,498 in 1973. This means that, as more and more hunters went into the field, hunter success rates steadily declined from the vicinity of 20 to 25 percent to between 10 and 14 percent.

An even more significant aspect of such statistical analysis is one that mere numbers can't measure. A sizable part of those "success" statistics are made up of serious and accomplished elk hunters who bag their elk every year; thus, the actual success rate for the average hunter is much lower than 10 to 14 percent and my totally unscientific estimate is that the true success rate for the average elk hunter is closer to 5 to 6 percent. That means that elk are even more difficult to get and thereby a more prized trophy than generally considered.

Upwards of 110,000 to 120,000 people ago afield in quest of elk nowadays, a statistic that has become more sharply definable as, in recent decades, license sales have been made specifically on the basis of species involved rather than a single license that enabled the holder to hunt several big game species.

Recent seasons also have seen an overall tightening up of regulations to protect the general elk population and to ensure quality, sustainable elk herds as, once again, statistics alone don't tell the whole story. Through much of the 1960s and into part of the 1970s, a hunter could take either a bull or cow elk in most hunting districts — particularly those west of the

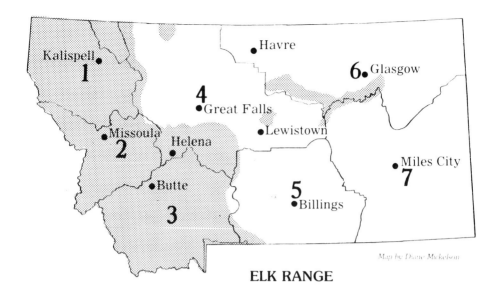

Kalispell
1

Havre

6. Glasgow

4
Great Falls

Lewistown

Missoula
2
Helena

Miles City
7

Butte
3

5
Billings

Map by Diane Mickelson

ELK RANGE

Continental Divide. Then, as hunter numbers increased, the kill was limited in most districts to bulls only and in others even restricted to branch-antlered bulls. Now elk populations are regulated by issuing cow permits in many districts on a drawing basis or, in some areas, a week-long period in which either cows or bulls can be taken. That's basically why the elk kill has remained constant while hunter numbers have increased.

Another building controversy of significance to elk hunters is herd constituency — the mixture not only of cows to bulls in any given herd or district, but the ratio of young bulls to older bulls and thereby the number of huntable animals in any given herd. Where spike bull seasons are closed, it's obvious that fewer elk will be taken in any given year and harvest statistics will directly reflect that limitation.

At face value, this controversy takes the shape of those who want to hunt for bigger, trophy bulls and those who don't care what size of an elk they get so long as they get meat. Actually, more is involved than who can take what size of bull or whether someone pursues meat or trophy. Ultimately the biological quality of a herd is affected by the type of seasons imposed upon a given district, but again no single, hard-and-fast rule can be applied everywhere. The impact of restrictive kill rules — generally called branch-antlered seasons — varies from area to area, largely because of variations in habitat and that all-important factor of elk security.

Biologists in the Montana Department of Fish, Wildlife and Parks describe the situation in terms of two factors: where elk security is inadequate and where it is adequate.

The Gravelly Range in southwestern Montana is a prime example of a range where elk security is inadequate. Here a shortage of cover, easy road access and heavy hunting pressure have resulted in a high elk harvest. Prior to the branch-antlered restriction in that area, most of the bulls harvested were spikes and few bulls were left in the herd following hunting season. Surveys on winter ranges showed very low calf crops and a high proportion of small, poorly developed calves; and research from other states suggested that this poor calf production may stem from the scarcity of mature bulls in the populations.

"The branch-antlered bull season allows more yearlings to survive the hunting season, resulting in improved calf production and survival," Glenn Erickson of the MDFW&P said in explaining why branch-antlered seasons have been adopted in some parts of the state. "This ultimately benefits the sportsman through a healthier, more productive elk herd."

In much of the more heavily timbered, less-roaded and thereby more inaccessible parts of the state, herd productivity is not a problem and branch-antlered bull seasons are generally less desirable from a hunter's point of view. When spikes are not harvested, there obviously will be more spikes on the winter range than when spikes are harvested. Again, Erickson explained that since most elk winter ranges are now supporting the desired numbers of elk, an increase in spikes on the winter range will probably necessitate a decrease in cows and calves. Thus, in the first few years of a branch-antlered bull season, an increase in antlerless elk permits — cows and calves — will be undertaken to reduce the cow-calf segment of the population. A price is paid for this adjustment, however.

"Eventually, because of fewer cows in the herd and fewer calves produced, the total harvest will be lower than that achieved by a general bull season," Erickson said.

Obviously, pursuing policies that provide for trophy animals results in a decline in the overall numbers of animals that can be taken from any given area. Erickson noted that ultimately the determination of that policy is in the hands of the hunters. "The department (MDFW&P) attempts to tailor regulations to meet both the biological needs of elk and the desires of sportsmen," he said. "With an abundance of high-quality elk habitat, the debate over branch-antlered bull seasons become irrelevant — hunters can seek the hunting experience that meets their 'ideal,' be it a record book bull or just good meat in the freezer. If elk security is steadily eroded, all elk hunters stand to lose. Only by maintaining quality elk habitat and adequate elk security can we ensure the continuation of the diverse hunting opportunities that we have enjoyed in the past."

Not only does the hunter have to decide where he or she will hunt elk, but also he or she must choose which part of the season to hunt — as well as the hunting method to be used. None of these are easy tasks. There are

Photo of a tremendous bull elk taken from the Horse Prairie country west of Dillon in 1977. Photo courtesy Jack Atcheson Jr.

many options, including early-season in the backcountry for rifle or bow but under conditions that generally require horses, with the bow and arrow (September through early October), early general hunting season when it's usually warm (late October through the first week of November), mid-season (middle two weeks of November) when anything can happen with the weather and snow is normal, and late season (usually the week of Thanksgiving Day) when both cold and snowy conditions can be experienced.

Kill statistics, again, don't give you a complete answer in terms of deciding when to hunt. In the northwestern and western districts approximately half the kill is made in the first week of the season, while in the more open and more accessible terrain of southern and southwestern Montana a bigger harvest comes late in the season.

There is also the issue of personal preference. The unpredictability of weather in November — it can be a mild, Indian-summer or a raging blizzard from day-to-day or for days upon end — inspires many individuals to get their hunting in early, before it becomes particularly arduous just to be outdoors. Others prefer the extremes of deep snow and cold; it does get animals moving from their high-country summer ranges to the winter ranges, and occasionally the hunter can ambush them on the trek between the two.

The how of hunting varies by virtue of personal preference and terrain, too. In most of the mountain country where elk secret themselves in timbered basins and draws, still hunting is the most often used technique;

this is usually done on foot, but often horses are utilized to cover more country. The still technique means the hunter will move quietly and slowly through the forest to slip up on the elk. It is particularly useful during the midday hours when the elk are bedded down and in mountainous terrain where the hunter can gain an altitude advantage over elk.

Closely associated with still hunting is the technique of stalking, which is commonly used in more open country where elk can be sighted in openings or along the edges of timber. The hunter then plans and executes a stalk on the elk, utilizing terrain and the single most important element in elk hunting — the wind — to get close enough to make a shot. This is a particularly good method when you can get a find vantage point to scan the countryside with field glasses or a spotting scope to locate and then sneak up on elk.

Wallow sites and associated wet areas are excellent places to locate game. Here's an example of one that several wildlife species, including elk, used.

An extremely popular method for the most hardy hunters, particularly in late season when the snow is deeper, is tracking — locating an elk's tracks in the snow and then simply following its trail until you catch up. The advantage of this method is that you know you're hunting a specific elk; it's a high-adrenalin form of hunting. The disadvantages are that it requires fairly good physical strength and stamina and you can be led a long and merry way over difficult terrain — elk often move several miles when spooked — under conditions that most often favor the elk.

Stand hunting isn't used as often for elk as it is for, say, whitetail deer or antelope, but it does work, particularly if you can locate a good watering hole or a prime wallowing site early in the season. Similarly, the ambush technique where you place yourself along a well-traveled route and shoot an elk as it moves to its bedding area from its early-morning feeding range, or vice versa, is a good technique if you've sufficiently scouted the area involved and know where to locate yourself to make that ambush.

Sometimes combinations of these techniques work best. I recall a hunt in the high, steep terrain of southwestern Montana. In most of this country, sagebrush covers the steep mountain slopes right up to the top of the ridges, where spindly Douglas-fir thickets take over on the north side of the ridges. Often elk can be located on the edges of these north-slope thickets. I'd been still hunting just after daylight, putting myself deep into

Photo by Neal Mischler

A fine trophy elk is caught in the sort of dense cover his species seeks out once hunting begins. Hunters occasionally encounter big bulls in open country, but most are found in cover like this.

the backcountry where I planned to utilize the spot-and-stalk technique if I didn't encounter elk on the way into the remote basin. Little did I realize as I worked my way to the high country that it would be a third technique, the ambush, that would provide me a nice five-point bull elk that day.

By midmorning I'd spotted a few mule deer, including one nice buck, feeding out in the open of a big, steep draw — but no elk. Finally I decided to climb a steep ridge to a rocky point, perhaps 1,000 feet above me, from which I could use field glasses to cover the entire basin, hopefully locate an elk and then work a stalk on it. As a bonus, I thought I might try to get at the big mule deer buck if things worked out since the rocky point was within 400 or 500 yards of the buck and my climb to the knob would keep me out of its sight.

It didn't work out like I had planned, however. When I got to the big rock, paused to collect my breath from the steep climb and eased myself into position along the rock I was in for a surprise. The herd of mule deer had disappeared. I must have spooked them somehow, I thought, though I knew my ascent to the rocky point had been well executed, quietly, out of sight and downwind from the deer. Then I picked up the sharp clatter of a hoof against a rock and immediately caught sight, a half mile up the draw, of a herd of elk working its way across the ridge. Apparently it had been the elk, and not me, that had spooked the deer.

Anyway, I watched the elk for a couple of minutes to determine their route and dropped back off the ridge to the north, into the dense Douglas fir and literally ran uphill as fast as I could on the steep terrain to close my distance on the elk. When I thought I was getting within range — I shoot a .270, so I don't like to shoot more than a couple of hundred yards — I slowed, caught my breath again, and eased to the edge of the timber at the top of the ridge. Sure enough, the elk were traveling single file along the scant trail, right toward my ambush site and a couple of minutes later the five-point bull fell to a shot placed behind his left shoulder.

Not only did I have a fine trophy and a winter's supply of meat, I had the memory of a hunt in which the three key elements of successful elk hunting had worked to perfection — the resourcefulness to use whatever technique conditions required, the adaptability to make changes in strategy and technique immediately, and, lastly, the most important ingredient and one I count on more often than I should, luck.

Then again, none of them would have worked if I hadn't put myself in good elk country to begin with — and that's basic to the success or failure of any kind of hunt. Good hunting begins with the preservation of good places for elk to live.

Chapter 4

Deer

When it comes to hunting deer in Montana, contradiction is the key word. Deer are found, literally, everywhere in the Big Sky country, particularly the most common of all Montana's big game animals, the mule deer. Still, both mule deer and their counterpart, the whitetail, tend to spend most of their time in pockets or small parts of their total range. Thus, while deer range encompasses the entire state, parts of Montana seem at times to be devoid of this most sought-after game animal.

Further, deer are both the easiest and most difficult big game animal to hunt and while that statement might seem contradictory, it isn't. Sheer numbers make deer easier to locate and kill than any of the big game animals; thus they are the easiest of the hunters' quarry to take. Simultaneously, those hunters who pursue the truly trophy bucks — whitetail and mule deer alike — find they've taken on extremely worthy challenges. The big, big bucks take full advantage of their natural attributes and the difficult-to-hunt terrain they live in to give trophy hunters the fits and — surprise — supreme joy even when the deer eludes the hunter and no kill is made.

Another contradiction is that while some deer will appear almost stupid as they bunch up in an open field or mountain meadow, others seem to possess almost supernatural wiles as they outsmart one hunter after another, year after year. In many hunting circles, the whitetail buck is seen as the supreme hunting trophy and the most difficult of hunting challenges. Thus is born the legend of the "Old Mossyhorn" buck, the monster trophy that somehow takes on bigger-than-life proportions and gives the sport of deer hunting a mystique equalled in hunting lore only by that of the marauding "Slewfoot" bear that somehow eludes the hunters' guns from year to year.

This mystique is particularly true regarding Montana's whitetail deer, which in recent years have taken on superstar status among a close-knit fraternity of trophy whitetail hunters who believe that the next world record whitetail is going to come from Montana. And that's part of the continuing contradiction: even though Montana has trophy mule deer throughout the state, its whitetail deer population boasts, proportionately, more trophy-size bucks of potential world-record class.

Photo by Ed Wolff
A second before he took off for the timber, and escape, a five-point mule deer buck is shown in a pose common to those who hunt these magnificent animals.

Montana is rife with trophy-size mule deer. From the big bucks of the upper Whitefish Mountain range to those of the Bitterroot and Sapphire Mountains (the state record comes from the Sapphires), on to the Missouri Breaks and the grassy ridges of the Ashland area in southeastern Montana, mule deer bucks sporting 20-inch-wide racks and larger are common. Still, Montana isn't noted as a producer of the really big, world-record-class trophy mule deer bucks. It is recognized, however, as a major and possibly the most outstanding trophy whitetail producer in the country. Only time will tell if that reputation is justified.

Montana is noted as a prolific producer of deer, period. Whitetail and mule deer are at all-time population highs in the 1980s, a factor that throughout the decade has provided excessively liberal deer seasons and harvest figures in excess of 100 percent. In fact, multiple tags have been available in some areas where the excessive deer populations required reductions to alleviate damage to agricultural land — though the drought of 1985 reduced that population somewhat.

Deer numbers are expected to stay high through the 1980s, according to Ron Marcoux, associate director of the Montana Department of Fish, Wildlife and Parks, who noted that deer management is more dependent on complications brought on by social factors rather than by biological problems. Two such "social factors" he cited for emphasis are hunter congestion and landowner tolerance of the increasing numbers of hunters in the field to accommodate the expanded, and necessary, deer harvest.

"We do everything we can to avoid conflicts, but some of our problems result from social impacts beyond our control," Marcoux said. "Since many deer are found on private land, the interrelationship of the sportsman and landowner is one of our biggest management issues."

The present high point in deer populations may have led to such problems, but no one in the hunting fraternity is lamenting the availability of increased hunting opportunities — particularly following puzzling declines in mule deer numbers in the mid-1970s. Hunting seasons then were drastically curtailed to accommodate a downswing in mule deer numbers that, unexplainably, struck not only Montana but most western states.

No such downswing occurred with whitetails. Indeed, the species seemed to expand its range in the 70s and biologists and hunter sightings generally confirm this. Eugene Allen, who in the 1970s was administrator of the wildlife division for the MDFW&P, added another insight, however. He suggested that records indicated the whitetails had steadily increased their range from 1940 to the 1970s, but that the decline in mule deer numbers in the early 70s made the presence of whitetails more noticeable.

"It's probably more true that what people perceived to be a whitetail increase in the late 1970s was really due to the fact that our mule deer population had really decreased," Allen said. "Thus a larger percentage of the deer seen in any given area was whitetailed when that really wasn't the case. Their numbers were the same, though we were seeing a larger percentage of whitetails in proportion to the total deer population."

Now, a decade later, both species are at the peak of their expansion and Montana deer hunting offers more than at any time in its history — given, of course, the limiting factor that many more people are vying for those animals. Old-timers might lament that hunting has become more competitive than it used to be, but no one can deny that Montana deer hunting offers something for everyone. There's at least one deer out there for everyone who wants to hunt and there are sizable tracts of land in Montana that, for one reason or another, are never trod by the hunter's foot.

Mule Deer

There has not been a time in recent human history in the place known as Montana when mule deer did not play an important role, either as a source of food, buckskin, recreational viewing and hunting, or, in earlier times, as a source for implements made from its bones and antlers.

Today the adaptable mule deer *(Odocoileus hemionus)* is Montana's most widespread big game animal. It ranges everywhere in the state from the dense forests of northwestern Montana where deep snows and heavy rainfall is common to the arid badlands of the eastern prairies and the high, park-like slopes of southwestern and southcentral Montana. It lives in the bottomlands and occasionally, like whitetail, on the very outskirts of many Montana communities. You'll find mule deer where it's dry, where it's wet, where it's steep and where it's flat, on ridges and rocky terrain that's so precipitous a human being has trouble staying on the side of the hill. Then, for good measure, you'll encounter mule deer in great

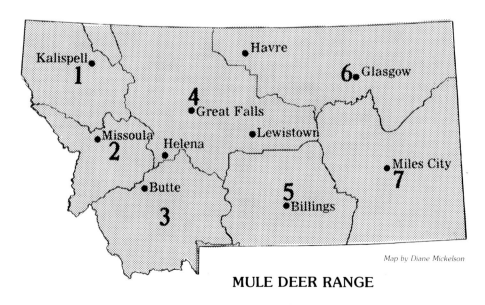

Map by Diane Mickelson

MULE DEER RANGE

numbers on tracts of flat prairie land so open and exposed that an antelope would be embarrassed to be found there.

Part of the mule deer's popularity is its omniscience. But it also, provides a quality hunting experience, particularly when it comes to hunting big, trophy bucks in the high, remote and generally inaccessible regions of either the mountain country or the Missouri Breaks. Those bucks are big, both of body and antler — many exceed 300 pounds in weight and antlers with 30-inch-plus spreads.

Most mule deer, however, are smaller than that. Bucks tend to range from 200 to 275 pounds, does 150 to 175. Their coats are brownish in the summer months and a lighter, grayish-brown in the winter. Their foreheads and briskets are dark, while chins, throats and rump patches are white. Tails are short and round with black tips that have led to them being called "blacktailed" deer which, while true, is misleading because two smaller subspecies of the mule deer are found in states along the West Coast and they are truly called blacktailed deer. Neither of the subspecies of blacktail deer range in Montana.

It is the set of very distinct, large, mule-like ears, however, that give the mule deer its name — some people, in fact, attribute the assigning of that reference to Meriwether Lewis, who recorded in his journals sightings of the species in Montana. Lewis wrote: "We have rarely found the mule deer in any except rough country. They prefer the open grounds and are seldom found in woodlands or river bottom." Whatever the case and whoever first labeled the species mule deer, it's understandable why the name stuck. The mule deer's ears are an absolute giveaway and often can be seen on the skyline like a beacon when no other part of the deer is visible.

A second characteristic of the mule deer that assists in immediate identification is its bounding, spring-like gait when running. Often it will do a spritely trot when startled or puzzled and then, when the puzzlement turns to alarm, the mule deer will literally explode in long, soaring bounces that seem to leave them hanging in mid-air but which, in reality help them cover a lot of country in a hurry.

The mule deer buck's antlers also are distinct from the whitetail's. The typical buck has four tines on each side and five if brow tines are present — they sometimes aren't — and the brow tines tend to be shorter than a whitetail's and also tip forward somewhat. A mule deer's antlers also fork equally rather than develop from a main stem as the whitetail's do.

Because of their wide variations in range, mule deer eat different things in different areas. Joe Egan, a wildlife biologist with the MDFW&P who has played a major role in the implementation of practices that helped restore mule deer habitat in Montana from its low point in the 1930s and 1940s and thus enabled its great recovery, detailed the mule deer's diet situation in the book *Game Management in Montana*.

"All wild animals need specific kinds of food and cover, and the mule deer is no exception," Egan wrote. "In late spring, summer, and early fall certain weed type plants are a necessity in the mule deer's diet. Leaves and twig ends of certain bushes are also eaten. With the approach and arrival of winter, the mule deer shifts almost entirely to specific types of brush for food. As new green growths of weeds appear in the spring, deer begin to use them. Also at this time deer use some grass. Food habit studies have shown beyond any doubt that grass is not used extensively by mule deer. Browse and weeds (forbs) are the mule deer's primary food. In Montana, the quality and quantity of browse (the winter food supply) is the factor most often limiting deer numbers."

Egan added that the list of food plants that must be present in both quantity and quality to support large numbers of deer varies only slightly from one part of the state to another. The main browse plants are mountain mahogany, bitterbrush, chokecherry, serviceberry, common and creeping juniper, mountain maple, evergreen and red stemmed Ceanothus, big and fringed sagebrush, silver sagebrush, skunkbrush, rabbitbrush and dogwood.

Photo by Neal Mischler

The pumping of adrenalin through a hunter's arteries is excusable when this sort of situation develops. Any one of these superb mule deer trophies would gladden the heart of the majority of deer hunters in the state.

With mule deer populations currently at a high level and everything looking good for the immediate future, the impression might well be that this has always been the case. That impression would be wrong. The mule deer, like almost every big game species in Montana, has had tough times.

From the earliest settlement times onward, mule deer grew more and more scarce in Montana and by the early 1900s restrictions had been imposed on their harvest. Not only were the deer taken for their meat and hides, but much of their former habitat — millions of acres, in fact — was converted to agricultural use.

Several milestones in the state's mule deer history are worth noting:

• By 1917 Dawson, Custer, Richland, Rosebud and Yellowstone counties in eastern Montana were closed to deer hunting after deer numbers plummeted.

• By 1921 15 counties, primarily in the eastern part of the state, were closed to hunting, again because of declines in deer numbers, and a limit of one buck deer was imposed on those areas still open to hunting.

• Mule deer remained scarce throughout the 1930s and game preserves were established on the premise of providing "seed stock" for repopulating adjacent areas.

• Some 1,286 mule deer were transplanted from western Montana to 16 sites in eastern Montana between 1943 and 1950. These helped bolster populations of mule deer that had already begun to respond to improving environmental conditions as much of the land that had been converted to agricultural use was abandoned after it proved unfit for such use. Original vegetation types began to reoccur on the sites and mule deer began to recover.

• Either-sex hunting seasons to curb growing deer populations began in the 1950s amidst considerable controversy but ultimately the public began to comprehend that such seasons were necessary to enable habitat improvement. The first statewide either-sex season occurred in 1958 and special early and late season hunts were begun in some areas to alleviate deer damage to agricultural crops.

• A mild decline in mule deer numbers occurred in the 1960s, followed by a peak in the early 1970s and then a drastic drop in the mid 1970s. This occurred throughout the western states and for reasons never really determined. Since the late 1970s the population of mule deer has been steadily increasing.

• The statewide deer harvest reached 134,000 in 1957 and then declined for a short period before reaching 136,000 in 1973 — the record harvest.

Hunting mule deer takes many forms all the way from "road hunting" — sighting of deer from a moving vehicle on forest or farm vehicle roads or jeep trails and then stopping and shooting them — to pure sight-and-stalk hunts for trophy mule deer bucks on high mountain ridges or in the breaks country.

Probably the two most commonly used techniques, however, are still hunting, particularly in the timbered parts of the state where it isn't easy to spot deer until you've gotten in quite close to them, and a technique well suited to the brushy draws of eastern Montana, a modified "drive" in which one hunter goes into a draw or coulee to drive the deer out ahead of him. Other hunters stationed along the edges of the coulee on either side then do the shooting when the deer are spooked out into the open.

A third method that works very well under most conditions, but is exceptionally efficient in two specific circumstances encountered in Montana, is the spot-and-stalk technique. This is very effective in the breaks country and even better in high, open or rocky mountain terrain. The method requires the use of field glasses — most hunters use something in the 7x35 range — to locate deer that are either feeding in the morning or traveling from a water source to their bedding area and then executing a stalk on them. More often, however, the deer are located, through the careful use of field glasses, bedded down after the morning feed. Then the hunter works in as close as she or he can for a shot.

Another method I personally enjoy because it offers a chance at truly trophy-size bucks is to track them in the snow of the late season in high country basins or the upper reaches of a mountain. Indeed, one of the most satisfying mule deer hunts I ever experienced occurred this way.

After hiking about two miles up a Forest Service trail in a canyon on the west side of the Bitterroot Mountains, I encountered a set of huge tracks in snow that was about knee deep and once I'd determined it was mule deer and not elk — the techniques of tracking the two in deep snow are not the same — I began a drama that took over four hours to unfold.

My best estimate was that the tracks were no more than an hour old (I came across them about 10 a.m.) and since they were fresh, it was likely that the buck would bed on a ridge or outcropping from which he'd have a commanding view of the surrounding terrain. Because the head of that canyon lay no more than three-quarters of a mile ahead of me and consisted of a gentle, constantly rising basin floor covered by a deep blanket of snow and fairly sparse clumps of alpine fir and an occasional spruce thicket, I was sure I'd jump the buck within an hour.

However, like I've found I'm prone to do in such situations, I vastly underestimated both the distances involved and the difficulty of the terrain. For one thing, as I moved to follow the buck's trail off the south-facing slope of the canyon, the snow got deeper and more difficult to move through. Two hours later, exhausted from struggling through thigh-deep snow, I crouched under the overhanging branches of a big spruce tree and broke out my lunch. I'd encountered no sign of life in the upper basin other than the mule deer's tracks and was ready to give up the hunt, but continued to scan a patch of timber about 400 yards away as I ate. I decided that, since it was the largest patch of cover in the entire upper basin, it was likely that the buck had bedded down there. I'd go that far, at least, and if I didn't jump the buck I'd head back down the canyon.

Then, just as I was hoisting my daybag to my shoulders, I caught sight of a small tree, in that clump of Douglas fir about 400 yards away, that was shaking violently. Once again I dug my field glasses out of the pack and focused them on the tree. Nothing. Then, wham, the tree shook again as if it would explode and a mule deer head with an incredible set of antlers popped into view — only to immediately disappear again. The buck **was** in that clump of trees and he **was** as big as I'd thought he might be! He repeated the raking again, and then again and again. I assumed he was raking his antlers as a function of the rutting period.

For another half-hour I watched him, realizing that to reach him I'd have cross a wide open snowfield. Only one lone, head-high Douglas fir stood between us halfway across the opening. Further, I knew that even getting to the cover of that lone fir would be extremely slow. The snow would be even deeper out in the open. Then I got a fix on the sapling the buck was raking and decided to move when the tree moved, assuming that the buck would be occupied during those moments. Each time he raked, I moved as quickly as I could toward him; each time he stopped, so did I. Finally, a half-hour later, I reached the small tree in the middle of the deep snowfield.

Then, abruptly, the raking stopped — or at least the tree ceased to move — and I could only guess that either the buck had bedded down or had spotted me and taken off. I waited for 10 minutes and then 20, wet and chilled from perspiration. But again, nothing. No movement. No noise. Only an eerie, high-country silence interrupted by my deep, oxygen-seeking breaths and a gentle sigh from a north wind gave any indication of life in the high basin.

By now the incline of the basin had put the thicket where the buck had been raking the tree right above me, about 200 yards away. Nothing but open snow lay between it and the tree that hid me. I decided I had to chance a dash — if you can call waddling through thigh-deep snow a dash — to the edge of timber and hope that I could make it without alarming the buck, assuming he had bedded and was still there.

So I waddled. Five minutes. Ten. Twenty or more. Completely exposed. And then I was at the edge of the timber. It was a 10- or 12-foot climb to the top of the small ridge that separated me from the site where I believed the buck to be and now, trying to regain my breath and my composure, I began a tedious, step-by-step ascent, my .270 at the ready. Then, just as I reached the top I stepped on and broke an unseen branch under my upper, or left, foot.

"Bad luck," I whispered to myself, but I was wrong. Immediately there was a stomping sound just ahead of me and the horns and head of that mule deer buck appeared 50 feet in front of me. In the split-second that it took for him to recognize what I was and begin to swing away, I'd got off my shot and he was down. It was only later, when my emotions had settled down after dressing him out and I'd begun the tedious task of getting him out of the basin, that I realized my luck had held to the end. If I'd stepped on and broken that branch with my right foot instead of the left, it would have been impossible for me to get a shot off in the millisecond the buck had given me. Bad luck, indeed. It was only the final episode in one of the most outstanding hunting experiences I've ever had, and now, as I write this, I can hear that twig snapping as clearly as I did on that supreme mule deer hunt several years ago.

Whitetail Deer

Whitetailed deer have been making steady gains in Montana over the last few decades, though it isn't likely that the "common deer," as Meriwether Lewis labeled many of the whitetailed deer his party killed, will ever surpass the mule deer in either distribution or numbers in the state.

For the last few decades, the kill of whitetail deer in Montana has hovered near 25 to 29 percent of the total deer harvest. Now that harvest

Photo by Frank R. Martin

A young but nonetheless exceptionally beautiful trophy, this whitetail buck is fairly typical in both body size and symmetry to those found in central Montana.

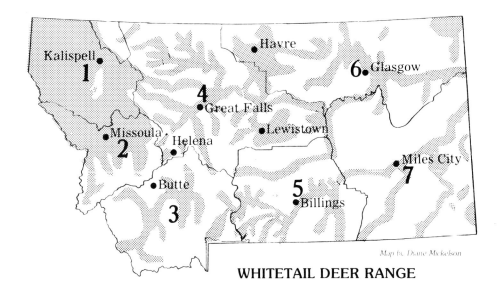

WHITETAIL DEER RANGE

Map by Diane Mickelson

has edged up to more than a third of the kill, 33.4 percent in 1984 and as much as 37 percent in other recent years. That trend is likely to continue, too, if whitetail continue to expand their range. Thus, the whitetail deer, always a significant part of the big game hunting picture in Montana, will grow in importance as two key factors involving its numbers in Montana merge — the expansion of the whitetail population and increasingly better access to private lands where most whitetails are found.

Whitetail deer are popular for a variety of reasons, but most notably among the vast majority of hunters because they have exceptionally palatable meat. Others prefer hunting whitetails because the the species — particularly the big, trophy-size buck — offers an exceptionally difficult-to-get, and therefore prized, trophy. In fact, some people believe the whitetail buck to be the supreme North American hunting challenge.

The latter point has led, over the last few years, to the emergence of a new hunting fraternity subculture in Montana — a group of fanatical whitetail deer hunters who believe that the next world record whitetail is going to come from Montana. Dr. Edward Wolff of Missoula, who has documented this phenomenon in his book *Hunting Trophy Whitetails,* estimates that as many as 50 individuals have either settled in Montana or come here each season on the premise that Montana offers the best chance of any state of providing big Boone & Crockett bucks.

Whether or not that assumption is true, the whitetail deer is one of Montana's "Big Four" game animals — sharing top billing with the mule deer, the elk and the antelope. Of these, only the mule deer is more widespread or provides more harvest numbers. For example, in 1984 hunters took 18,478 elk in Montana, 28,588 antelope, 112,873 mule deer — and 56,761 whitetail deer.

Much of that whitetail harvest occurs west of the Continental Divide where the species is found just about everywhere from the bottomlands of the Bitterroot Valley northward to heavy concentrations in Flathead, Lincoln and Sanders counties.

Other major whitetail deer populations are found in the river bottoms east of the Continental Divide, particularly along the Yellowstone, Missouri and Milk Rivers, in the Longpine Hills near Ekalaka, the Bear Paw Mountains at Havre and an exceptionally thriving population in the Snowy Mountain foothills near Lewistown Two areas of growing significance to the whitetail deer hunter are the Rocky Mountain Front — that area east of the Continental Divide north of Highway 200 and south of Glacier Park — and the river bottoms of southwestern Montana, particularly in the Sheridan, Ennis, Whitehall, Bozeman and Livingston areas.

In commenting on the former, Harley Yeager, information officer for the Montana Department of Fish, Wildlife and Parks in Great Falls, noted that whitetail have moved into much of the area along the Front. He said there also are considerable numbers of whitetail in the Sweet Grass Hills. LeRoy Ellig, supervisor of the department's Region Three headquartered in Bozeman, said that whitetail deer have been expanding their numbers in that area over the past 25 years.

"Once the whitetail was a curiosity in our area," Ellig said, "but now they're found in substantial numbers in every river bottom. Whitetails are very secretive and you've got to have substantial numbers before people know they're around.

The whitetail deer *(Odocoileus virginianus)* is a stunningly beautiful animal. Its color ranges from reddish-brown in the summer to a softer grayish-brown in the winter; each is offset by a white underbelly, a white patch on the neck and white markings on the muzzle and around the eye. However, its most readily identifiable characteristic is the one that gave the whitetail its name — a foot-long, white tail that it raises and flashes when alarmed. This flag, or flaum as it is more properly called, is a common sight when whitetail deer have been spooked. They appear to use it as a signal to other deer.

Mature whitetail bucks can be hefty. They commonly weigh 250 pounds or more, as compared to 160 to 180 pounds for does and younger bucks. Both sexes have a small scent gland outside on the lower hind leg. The whitetail buck's antlers are distinct from the mule deer's in that they have a main beam from which the tines, usually three to five, project upward to create a beautifully symmetrical rack.

The whitetail is a generally secretive species that favors heavily timbered or brushy areas, though it is much more adaptable than the mule deer and seems to have adjusted to living in close proximity to man. In fact, the whitetail is found on the outskirts of most Montana communities as well as in more remote — though most often timbered — areas.

A fine whitetail buck, commonly found in many of Montana's valley bottoms and almost everywhere in the state's river bottoms, was taken by Donna Copenhaver of Ovando near her home — and it was her first deer too!

Wherever they're found, the whitetail is extremely cunning; bedded bucks have been known to stay perfectly still as hunters passed within a few feet of them and then rise to sneak quietly away.

The whitetail is a prolific species. So long as the species has adequate habitat, does tend to have twin, and sometimes triplet, fawns. This, in part, may account for the steady expansion whitetail have enjoyed in Montana since the 1940s. Equally important, however, has been the fact that most whitetail populations generally are both undanderharvested — factors brought on by two key factors. These are the species' secretive habits, and thereby its ability to elude hunters, and the fact that in many parts of the state it exists on private land where hunter access is limited.

So critical is this latter factor that the Montana Department of Fish, Wildlife and Parks and many agricultural and sportsman's groups are working to achieve better access to private lands where whitetail numbers have increased to the point that they've become a bother to ranchers. An estimated 75 percent of the whitetail deer harvest in Montana comes from private lands.

Incidentally, this isn't a new problem. In 1970, Gene Allen of the Montana Department of Fish, Wildlife and Parks, wrote that the "chronic problem of whitetail management is obtaining an adequate harvest, particularly in rugged terrain and on private land where hunting is restricted."

Even in western Montana where considerable numbers of whitetail deer are found on public land, access to private land to hunt the species can be difficult. In the Bitterroot Valley where I live and which, incidentally, supports an incredible whitetail deer population, much of the land supporting whitetail is closed to hunting, period. Don't bother to ask, as one sign just north of Stevensville states. Most, however, can be hunted upon requesting permission and that ultimately is to the benefit of landowners who need whitetail numbers controlled and hunters who utilize the meat.

The methods of hunting of whitetail deer in Montana vary greatly from area to area and, naturally, by the weapons used to hunt them. In the mountainous or brushy, hilly country of western Montana, the still hunting method is most common. Bowhunters commonly use blinds or tree stands in the river bottoms and other areas where the whitetail inhabit amazingly dense, brushy terrain. Seldom are the spot-and-stalk technique or the true drive common to the East used in Montana.

I grew up in northwestern Montana and, as a youth, honed my hunting skills on whitetail deer. Consequently, I learned the art of still hunting, of quietly stalking deer in heavily-timbered terrain and of being ever-alert for the sudden movement of an ear or patch of color, particularly white. And I doubt that I'll ever forget the counsel my grandfather gave me once, on a heavily timbered ridge near the small town of Olney in northwestern Montana. I can't forget it because it worked to perfection then and it has worked numerous times since — as it must have for him many times before he passed it on to me. He told me how to move along the ridge to take advantage of the lay of the land and a whitetail buck's habits. Then came the advice that is, to me, the hallmark of the good whitetail deer hunter. "Go as slow as you can," he said, "and then cut that in half."

Another basic is understanding the tendencies of the whitetail to stay put in a fairly small geographic area and to be loners. Whitetail are what is known as a homey species. They live out their lives in a fairly small area, often migrating only when weather forces them to lower country or areas with less snowfall. Further, the big bucks tend to keep off by themselves, in heavy brush or on ridges where they have commanding views of the surrounding terrain and easy escape from danger.

Whitetail also have nocturnal tendencies, meaning that they perform a lot of their livelihood activities — like feeding and traveling — at night. Thus, the hunter often has to pursue them into their bedding areas in the daytime and that is a primary reason for both the difficulty, and the challenge, of hunting whitetail deer. It is a species that knows how to take care of itself.

Chapter 5

The Antelope

For much of this century, the antelope in Montana and elsewhere was a species in dire trouble. From population estimates of 40 million over a range that extended from the tablelands of Mexico to the high plains of Canada and the Mississippi to Oregon and Washington, the species declined to a point that a special survey conducted by state and federal conservation agencies in 1922-24 showed that only 26,600, and possibly as few as 15,000, antelope remained in 16 western states. In Montana that estimate showed antelope numbers dipped as low as 3,000 from more than 2.5 million in the 1800s.

Now more than 25,000 are harvested each year in Montana and the antelope has become one of the great wildlife success stories precisely because sportsman-funded work went into saving them. Antelope have become, in terms of the number of hunters who go afield after them and the number of animals harvested, the second major wildlife species in Montana; deer are first.

The pronghorn antelope *(Antilocapra americana)* is uniquely a North American animal. It is found nowhere else in the world and from the first sighting of them by members of the Lewis and Clark Expedition to today it has fascinated people with both its fleetness of foot and graceful beauty. The antelope, called by the Indians the "runner of the plains," is an exceptionally striking, even beautiful, creation. Consider, for example this description by a nameless wildlife writer in a U.S. Department of Interior bulletin on the antelope:

"The rich brown coat lightens almost to a creamy white on the under part of the body, the sides of the face, and on the rump patch. The dark brown to black of the mane extends forward on each side of the neck and two broad white bands cross the throat. The male has a black mask over most of his face. The buck raises the long hairs of the mane when he is angry or when 'posing' — which is a peculiarity of the antelope, especially the males, and is seen even in very young fawns.

"The buck is a small creature, standing not more than 36 to 38 inches at the shoulder. Full-grown, he seldom exceeds 120 pounds; the doe is still smaller. His horns are hollow, covering a bony core, and pronged. The buck's horns extend well above his ears. The female has small horns or none. The hollow horn is dropped normally in early winter and grows back by summer. The antelope matures early and the life span is relatively short."

Antelope are found today throughout the eastern two-thirds of the state and in a few locations west of the Continental Divide, though only one very small district there is open to the taking of a limited number of the species. Even that season is, however, a tremendous indicator of the incredible recovery antelope have made in Montana.

From its low point in the 1920s when just 3,000 were distributed over 44 areas in central and southwestern Montana, the antelope population increased steadily from 10,600 in 1937 to about 75,000 in 1965. In 1941 transplanting began as a means of re-establishing the antelope over its former range; 3,554 antelope were released in 33 areas where none existed. In nine other areas transplants supplemented small, existing herds. Natural expansion of their distribution resulted and today the species is widespread throughout Montana's prairie country.

Antelope require specific vegetation types during various seasons of the year; like any species of wildlife, habitat is the key to their status. It is important to realize that while their decline in the opening decades of this century was partly due to their use as food by settlers, the conversion of their former native habitat to cultivation by homesteaders also contributed to their massive number reductions. Then came the great drought of the 1930s and homesteaders by the hundreds abandoned the dry country. The once-cultivated fields reverted back to vegetation more favorable to antelope, even the early succession that was comprised mostly of weeds, and with additional food and spaces antelope numbers increased steadily over the next several decades.

Obviously the antelope population will never reach the numbers of presettlement times, but management efforts today, which are intended to balance antelope numbers with agricultural land use, have led to fairly stable and widespread population levels.

Pronghorn antelope are best served by open, rolling sagebrush grasslands relatively free of human encroachment. These lands are generally used about half of the year by antelope, especially in the winter months when pronghorns feed extensively on various sagebrush species.

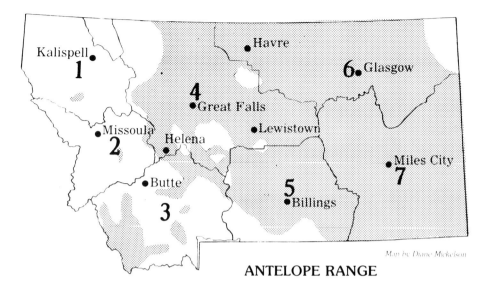

ANTELOPE RANGE

Map by Diane Mickelson

Vegetation types such as cropland, meadow and grassland receive little or no use during this period. During summer antelope utilize a diversity of plants, concentrating on mesas located in depressions and/or along creek bottoms. Preferred succulent vegetation persists longer there than on dry uplands where the sagebrush-grassland type occurs. Important forage plants in summer include fringed sagewort, longleaf sagebrush, three-leaved milkvetch, alfalfa and yellow sweetclover.

The hunting of antelope is likely more popular today than at any time in Montana's history. For a long time the pronghorn was largely ignored as a game animal or food source; neither the trappers nor Indians used it unless necessary. Other wildlife species were more palatable and abundant. Then came the settlers and homesteaders who, of necessity, used it for meat even though antelope meat can vary from being good to very bad from animal to animal.

Many hunters pursue antelope for their meat, however, and thousands are taken each year for that purpose — particularly does and young bucks. Others hunt them for the sheer excitement of the sport which, when approached with the notion of taking a fine trophy, can lift the endeavor of hunting to high drama.

Antelope live in open country and the best way to hunt them under conditions of fair chase is to locate a desired animal and make a stalk on it. And because antelope are blessed with both a awesome speed and incredible eyesight, the challenge of getting within a decent rifle shot of them can be extremely rewarding.

Sure, it's possible to "hunt" antelope from a vehicle and because open ground is often involved where antelope are sighted, that takes place a lot. But either the chasing of antelope in vehicles and then shooting them or following them cross-country in a fourwheeler is unsporting and also is doing more to undo the future of antelope hunting than any single factor — simply because landowners don't like what such methods do to their rangeland.

Bart O'Gara, leader of the Montana Cooperative Wildlife Research Unit and an internationally respected authority on hunting, put it as succinctly as can be in an article he did for **Montana Outdoors** magazine: "Over the long haul, the tolerance of landowners will determine how much land will be available, both to pronghorns and to hunters. I have talked with ranchers who would like to be rid of antelope; some were altering their fences and watering tanks to eliminate pronghorn populations. Competition for forage and damage to standing grain were occasionally given as reasons, but antelope hunters were the rancher's main complaint. Hunting without permission, leaving gates open, littering, shooting in the vicinity of livestock, and driving offroad across ranges and pastures were common offenses. Slob hunters endanger both the sport and (to a lesser extent) the animals themselves. This is unfortunate and ironic, because an antelope hunt is the ideal situation for teaching a young sportsman the ethics of hunting, the close stalk, the clean kill."

The first thing you need to hunt antelope in Montana is a permit, which is available by drawing and not that difficult to obtain. In recent years upwards of 65-70 percent of those applying were successful in getting a permit. In some districts where antelope numbers are higher than desired, in fact, multiple permits are available. Once you've drawn a permit you're allowed to purchase an additional tag to bag an extra antelope.

In 1984, 56,282 individuals applied for antelope tags. Sixty-nine percent (39,080) were successful. The catch is that some districts are extremely competitive because of their proximity to population centers and accessibility to good hunting land. Other districts that require long travel distances, particularly those in the easternmost part of the state, often do not have enough applications to cover the permits available. In those cases, the extra tags generally are made available on a first-come, first-serve basis.

The antelope season generally begins in early October and extends for approximately five weeks. The licenses generally are valid for either sex unless otherwise specified, but additional tags usually are limited to doe and fawn antelope.

Since antelope hunting resumed in Montana in 1943 when 750 permits were issued and 553 antelope were killed, both the number of permits issued and the kill increased to a point that has been fairly stable in the 1980s — more than 50,000 applications for about 35,000-39,000 permits and a take of approximately 25,000 animals.

In addition to your permit, one other prehunt condition is advisable to successful antelope hunting — get permission first if you plan to hunt on private land. That's a requirement of Montana law and **the** major offense cited by game wardens in Montana. Enough said!

A handsome critter indeed, the pronghorn or antelope is a respected and heavily-hunted Montana big game animal. Herds of these keen-sighted and fleet-footed animals have been fairly stable in Montana in recent years, but the species is susceptible to fluctuating population levels.

Now, to the actual hunt. The basic procedures are to either sight and then stalk a trophy, waiting in ambush at a fence crossing site or watering hole, flagging, or walking a buck down. Of these, the stalking probably takes the least time and energy and it is easily undertaken.

Often you'll encounter antelope while passing through an area in your vehicle. Should that occur, simply drive on without changing your speed or motor noise to the first place you pass out of the antelope's sight. Then take your field glasses and rifle, study the terrain and wind and try to work with the landscape to get within shooting distance of the trophy you want. This may appear difficult since you generally see antelope in open country, but even the "flat" prairie environment consists of hills and bullocks or depressions or gully-washer stream beds into which you can drop to keep out of sight as you move in on a herd of antelope.

Occasionally you'll encounter large herds with a trophy you'd like among them. In these cases, you often can place yourself in a position ahead of the direction the herd is moving and simply wait for your trophy to come within shooting distance. This sight-stalk-wait-shoot process works particularly well in places where the terrain is fairly broken and there's some brush cover or deeply-carved water drainage routes.

Several years ago, for example, I was hunting antelope south of Dillon when I spotted a herd of 100 or more antelope lazily feeding from my right to left, across what appeared to be a totally open, flat sagebrush bench. I tested the wind and determined that it would take me a couple of hours to crawl through the sagebrush to get ahead of them — just to get a shot at a nice but fairly-young buck that was feeding on the other side of the herd from me. I hadn't crawled more than a few yards, however, when I came to a narrow and shallow ditch carved out of the dry earth by spring runoff water. I slipped into the trench and within 10 minutes had placed myself both ahead of and downwind from the herd; a half hour later I made an easy 75-yard shot on the buck.

Long shots are a rule rather than the exception when hunting antelope, though I personally prefer to get within 125 to 150 yards and will work exceptionally hard — including arduous belly-crawling through sagebrush and around, not over, that every-present enemy, the prickly pear cactus — to get to a spot where I can be sure of my shot. Whatever rifle you use, it should be flat shooting, accurately sighted and have a sling. It's also best to use one equipped with a 4X scope or better. Most antelope hunters consider binoculars of 7X or more a necessity and if you're after trophy animals I'd recommend that you use a good spotting scope, too.

Those are basics. Some hunters also advise that you carry knee pads and gloves for protection against rocks and sagebrush while crawling your way through. Some also carry a small stick, or tripod, to steady their rifles on long shots. A canteen or bottle of water is a necessity. Often you'll have to spend several hours making a stalk or moving from one location to another as the antelope move, and generally when you hunt antelope you're in extremely dry country.

Most antelope are taken the first week of the season when the animals are less spooky and not inclined to take flight as a vehicle approaches and even stops. Many hunters, however, wait for that initial mass harvest of the animals to end and go afield for the sport of taking a trophy under more difficult field conditions — testing their sighting and stalking skills with animals that aren't as easy to approach. If you decide to try this challenge, plan to give your hunt a little more time. In open country a stalk can take a half a day or longer.

Another fascinating way to hunt antelope is to literally walk them down. Once spooked the pronghorns are fairly hard to approach and it's unlikely that you'll get closer than 500 or 600 yards before the one you want gets nervous and ready to take flight. Usually he'll run out of sight, a half mile or two in one direction or another. The hunter's task then is to test his or her own endurance by briskly hiking the same way.

Use extreme caution when coming to the crest or lift of land behind which the antelope disappeared. It usually will change directions to get in a better position to keep you in sight, so keep that in mind. When you do crest the sight barrier, slow your speed to a walk and proceed to a spot downwind of the animal. Remember, you now are close to that fidgety antelope and you know he's going to take off again. The catch is that each time you do this crazy stunt the antelope will let you get a little bit closer — 10 yards, even 20 or 30 yards. Finally, after working this routine upwards of a dozen times you're within that magical 300-250-yard barrier and can make a good rifle shot. Just be sure to make your shot quickly when you decide it's time to do so. By now the antelope is accustomed to your slow pace and stopping will again put it on edge.

Obviously this sort of tactic requires a considerable expenditure of energy and good physical conditioning. It also takes time, often six to eight hours because you can hike as much as a dozen miles to accomplish your goal — which is the taking of a nice trophy antelope buck.

What constitutes a trophy antelope? Without getting into the old "in the eye of the beholder" argument, let's look at what you can expect to encounter. A two-year-old usually carries thin horns about 13 inches long with small prongs. Lots of hunters are satisfied with heavier horns 14 inches in length. Anything over 15 inches is very good and many of this size are taken in Montana each year. Sixteen-inch horns are more rare but they are there to be had and if you get a set it makes a fine trophy.

The idea of trophies can be overworked, however, and I'm partial to the opinions expressed on that subject by two hunters I greatly admire. One is the aforementioned Bart O'Gara. The other is my 24-year-old son, Bruce, who has muscular dystrophy and hunts from a wheelchair.

"The trophy records are interesting and serve as standards for comparison," O'Gara said. "Many of the highest scoring heads are really freaks of nature, however, and hunters should not feel that heads that fail to make the book are second-rate trophies. An average buck — if hunted on foot, stalked fairly and dropped painlessly with one shot — is more of a trophy than the largest head in the world, if taking that head involved pure luck or an unsporting hunt. I keep small and medium-sized horns and antlers that remind me of enjoyable and exciting hunts."

For Bruce the situation was expressed on a hunt a couple of years ago in the prairie country north of Jordan. He bagged an antelope buck with horns that just made 15 inches, making a nice shot across 250 yards. To him it *was* a world record and I remember his joy at that moment as being worth more than anything a person could buy or what a listing in any record book would accomplish.

We had good field glasses with us that day, however, and we knew he was shooting at a fairly nice buck. But like most antelope hunters, we didn't know exactly how nice it was because it is fairly hard to determine the size of an antelope's horns under field conditions. Further, conditions vary from animal to animal in that while one might have good length, the base of its horns are small. Another might have poorly-pronged tops, and so on, and while I prefer to be choosy I've come to the conclusion that if I feel positive about a buck I go after it. Otherwise, I leave it and seek another.

Judging antelope at a distance might be difficult, but there are methods of coming close — and always, if you're truly after trophies, you'll want a good spotting scope to really get a fix on things. Short of that, remember that an antelope's ear is about six inches long and a buck's head is about 12 to 13 inches long. If the horns are somewhat longer than the buck's heads, you've got the makings of a fine trophy — but there are other considerations. The size of the horn base and the length of the prong are important. So is the curve of the hook. A rule of thumb is that nicely-defined horns the length or more of the head make a good and possibly even record-class trophy, assuming that the prongs and the hooks are similarly large.

One thing to remember if you're more interested in meat than you are in the trophy, antelope are basically a very small animal. Not only do they constitute a small target to shoot at, but even the average buck doesn't have a lot of heft. The largest ever recorded by the Department of Fish, Wildlife and Parks was 160 pounds live weight and 121 pounds dressed weight. The average buck more likely would dress out just under 100 pounds; does are much smaller.

Field care of antelope is especially important. Field dress the animal immediately upon kill and while not all hunters mind the musky odor of the animal's hide, most recommend that it also be skinned in the field and placed in clean meat bags. Place the meat where it will both cool and stay clean. If you're some distance from a vehicle and have to leave the carcass in the field for a period of time, leave it belly down both to facilitate drainage and to protect it from birds.

Often, the Indian summer period of October when antelope season opens is extremely warm during daytime hours. Warm temperatures require extra care to prevent meat spoilage, so it's important to cool the carcass as soon as possible after the kill. The best thing is to get it into an ice chest or a cooler, but if this isn't possible hang it in a shady, cool spot — a task easier said than done in some treeless antelope country.

Your chances of bagging an antelope are better than they are for any of the big game animals hunted in Montana. In 1983, for example, 96 percent of the hunters afield for antelope took them. As a means of comparison, consider that deer hunters scored 70 percent, elk hunters 16 percent, moose hunters 85 percent and bear hunters only 14 percent.

Chapter 6

Bear and Mountain Lion

For an animal as plentiful and widespread as it is in Montana, the black bear isn't hunted that extensively. And yet the black and its larger, more famous kin, the grizzly, both attract considerable attention in the Big Sky Country.

Black bear hunting has actually declined in recent years even though the harvest has stayed at about the same level, indicating that while the total number of hunters afield for bear is down, the people after them are more serious about it.

For example, in 1983 13,062 individuals hunted black bear in the spring and fall seasons. They took 1,820 bear for a success rate of 13.9 percent. In 1979, 17,121 hunters in the two seasons took 1,830 bear, a success rate of 10.6 percent. Over the past 40 years, the harvest has fluctuated between 1,400 and 2,100 bear per year.

Even so, black bear hunting in Montana has climbed in popularity to fourth place in terms of the total number of hours spent in quest of an animal — behind elk, mule deer and whitetail deer.

Mike Aderhold of the Montana Department of Fish, Wildlife and Parks, writing in that agency's magazine *Montana Outdoors* in early 1984 said that statistics show that in 1981 black bear provided 89,472 days of hunter recreation — more than antelope, bighorn sheep, moose, mountain goat, grizzly bear and mountain lion combined.

Black bear are widespread in Montana with their habitat being continuous from the timbered western part of the state to the wooded foothills east of the Continental Divide. In addition, the black bear is found in timbered regions in the central and southern part of the state. Officials estimate their current numbers at somewhere between 2,600 and 3,000. The black bear population is believed to have peaked in the mid-1970s at about 3,400 bears.

Hunters can look for fluctuations and tightening of the black bear season if current trends continue. Seasons already have been shortened to compensate for increased road access and lack of security for the bears in much of northwestern Montana. The seasons have been split into spring and fall periods to control hunting pressure; at this writing there is debate over whether to shorten or possibly even close the spring season.

The best time to hunt black bear is the spring, when they rouse from their winter's sleep and are dependent on food available in the more open, south-facing slopes and slide areas. A good way to hunt them at this time of the year is to glass these areas early in the morning as the annuals green early and provide the bear a ready and easily-obtainable source of food. Hunters often travel old, overgrown roads and walk or drive until reaching an avalanche chute in high country or those open, south-facing slides. They stop for half an hour or so glassing an open area, which is then covered with bright, new green growth. If no bear appears, the hunters move on to the next open area and repeat the process.

The best time of day to hunt bear is from dawn to about 9 a.m. and again in the afternoon from about 3 or 4 p.m. until dark. Bear don't feed much at midday, so that time period is usually nonproductive.

No one can predict exactly which period is best in any given year to hunt the black bear, but mid-April to mid-May is usually it. Once the bears have moved out of the slide and open areas and into the heavier timber, it is more difficult to locate them and thus the harvest declines. In the fall, the take increases again but hunter success improves only because there are more people afield hunting and most fall hunters take bear as an extra while hunting elk or deer.

Dr. Charles Jonkel, an internationally famous bear researcher at the University of Montana in Missoula who pioneered much of the bear research work in the country, recommends May 20 to June 10 as the best hunting period for black bear. "Most of the bear are out then, and the trees and shrubs have not leafed out yet, giving the hunters a better view of the dark figures on the hillsides," Jonkel said.

Big adult bores are the first out of their dens, though starving one and two-year-olds may be out foraging for food, too. They're hungry at this time of the year because they do not eat during their winter sleep; big males can lose up to 100 pounds. Because of their hunger, this also is the time of year when the bear conflicts most with man — in their search for food, bear raid dumps and garbage sites and other places in close proximity to human habitation. When that occurs, the offending bears normally are either killed or trapped and transplanted.

Season dates vary around the state for both the spring and fall seasons,

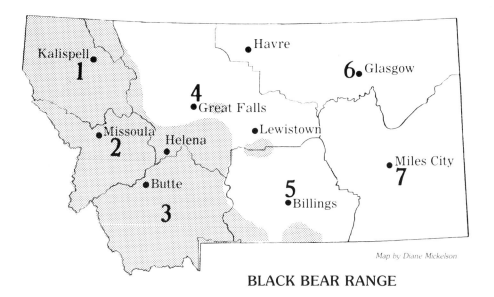

Kalispell
1

Havre

6. Glasgow

4
Great Falls

Missoula
2

Helena

Lewistown

Miles City
7

Butte

3

5
Billings

Map by Diane Mickelson

BLACK BEAR RANGE

so hunters are advised to check current regulations carefully. For example, in 1984, seasons in some areas were from April 15 to May 31 and others were from April 15 to May 25, another was from April 15 to May 31, and still another from April 15 to June 15. The same held true for the fall seasons. They varied from Sept. 8 to Nov. 25 and from Oct. 21 to Nov. 15, so you'll want to make sure you've got it right from district to district with an up-to-date hunting map.

Incidentally, in Montana it is illegal to bait bear or to hunt them with dogs — both factors that would increase the harvest and which are used in many other states.

Some of the hunting regions recommended by biologists in the Department of Fish, Wildlife and Parks are the Swan Valley, the South and Middle Forks of the Flathead River, the Whitefish Range, St. Regis River area and the Thompson Falls area west of the Continental Divide. East of the divide, the upper Yellowstone Valley and the Little and Big Belt Mountains afford good bear hunting.

Bear limits have been fairly constant throughout the history of regulated hunting in Montana — one per year of either sex. Cubs and females with cubs may not be taken. (Cubs are defined as the young of the year.) Prior to 1967, a license was issued simply for one bear per year and that bear could be either black or grizzly. Now separate licenses are issued for each species.

Hunters who take black bear normally do so for the pelt and yet several taxidermists I've talked with have lamented that many of the pelts they get aren't properly cared for in the field.

Such care begins immediately upon making the kill. Skin the animal out as soon as possible and remove the fat from the flesh side in the process. The cut along the belly should extend up through the chin to facilitate the removal of the hide. All bones should be removed from each foot, if not at the time of skinning, as soon as possible afterwards. Otherwise, hair on the feet will later slip.

Other critical steps at the time of skinning include severing the ear cartilage flush with the head muscles and carefully — very carefully — skinning the cape from the eyes and nose area. After the hide is off, allow it to cool and rub several pounds of salt into all parts of the fleshy side of the hide. The hide then can be rolled and should be taken to a taxidermist as soon as possible. Two cautions: never roll an unsalted hide unless it is to be frozen, and never leave any hide lying in direct sunlight.

One new requirement — it used to be voluntary — is to "turn in" a tooth from the skull of any bear taken. That tooth is used by biologists to develop age structure information of bear populations throughout the state and ultimately aid in management decisions, such as season setting and bag limits.

A major situation threatening bear hunting in Montana surfaced in 1984 — that of hunters mistaking grizzlies for black bear during the spring season. There is no spring season on the grizzly, which has a much more restricted season because it is listed as a threatened species by the federal government and it is hunted under rigidly controlled policies set by the state of Montana to allow sport hunting for a limited number of the big bears while ensuring the stability of their overall population.

It is a debate of major significance to the hunter because it involves controversies of jurisdiction — the state, which traditionally has responsibility for wildlife management, and the federal government, which enforces laws such as the Endangered Species Act — and disagreements within the conservation movement as to whether grizzlies should be hunted. The latter has led to the threat of legal action by such groups as the Defenders of Wildlife, which in recent years has taken on a much more obvious anti-hunting bias in its approach to the grizzly situation.

One way hunters can help this situation is to do considerable study — before they go in the field — of the differences between the two species. To help in this cause, a chart and drawings provided by the Montana Department of Fish, Wildlife and Parks is reprinted at the end of this chapter.

Grizzlies are hunted in Montana under strictly controlled regulations that allow the killing of only 25 bears per year, whatever the cause of death. That means that when the quota of 25 bears is reached either by hunters or nonhunters, the season is closed. For example, this quota was reached fairly early in 1984 — on Saturday, Oct. 20, west of the Continental Divide for a portion of the quota and Thursday, Oct. 25, east of the Divide.

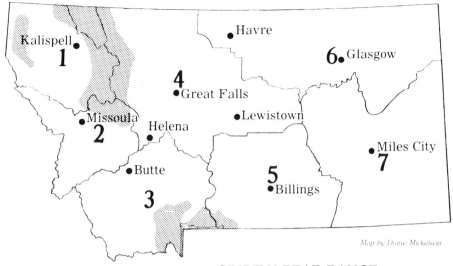

GRIZZLY BEAR RANGE

Jim Flynn, director of the Montana Department of Fish, Wildlife and Parks, explained why the 25-bear limit is set: "The two major grizzly populations in Montana are associated with lands within and adjacent to Glacier and Yellowstone National Parks. In the northwestern part of Montana, grizzly range includes the Bob Marshall, Scapegoat and Great Bear Wilderness areas. Hunting is used as a management tool in this ecosystem where the annual removal of grizzlies is limited to 25 bears (for all of Montana). This quota includes all known man-caused mortalities including hunting, marauders and those taken by poaching or otherwise illegally killed.

Grizzly hunters know the possibility exists each year that the season will be closed early and yet so prized is the grizzly as a trophy that each year they plunk down their license fees — $50 for residents and $300 for nonresidents, plus a $25 grizzly trophy license — even though there is no refund if the season is prematurely closed.

Most seasons, of course, are not. It just happened that in 1984 there were exceptionally large numbers of grizzlies killed by poachers and others in nonhunting situations.

Look for the grizzly controversy to be around for a while, even though cooler heads like the widely respected Dr. Charles Jonkel advocate continuance of the controlled seasons administered by the state rather than by federal bureaucracies. Jonkel believes that hunting actually helps the grizzly's interests and fears that debate over the hunting issue will detract from other critical needs of the bear — habitat protection and all too easy human access to grizzly country. Hunting also serves to keep the bears truly wild and helps maintain grizzly numbers at levels where conflicts with humans are kept to a minimum.

IDENTIFYING BEAR SPECIES

Black or Grizzly Bear?

If you plan to hunt either black bear or grizzly in Montana, contact the Montana Department of Fish, Wildlife and Parks (See address listings in Appendix A) or a license agent to obtain a copy of a wallet-sized pamphlet detailing bear characteristics.

Black Bear
1. Highest point of back is well back of shoulders. No prominent shoulder hump.
2. In profile, muzzle is long and straight.
3. Front claws dark colored, relatively short and well-curved.

Grizzly Bear
1. Highest point of back is muscular hump over front shoulders.
2. In profile, brow gives a "dished" look to face. Not as well defined in yearlings.
3. Front claws are up to 4" long or longer, and slightly curved. Front claws are light colored and can be sometimes observed from great distances.

Ruff of long hair in spring and fall

He believes that management considerations for hunting grizzly are sound, though indirect and based on a variety of data.

Jonkel pointed out that game management by legislation, rather than by professionals, is a poor approach but when professionals mess up the job that is too often the way things are done. "In the end, however, the animals suffer unnecessarily. It is important, therefore, that the state manage the grizzly carefully," he said. "At the state level, it is much easier to remain sensitive to all viewpoints and the needs of the local people and local resources. In the long term, the state can remain much more abreast of concerns by the rancher about livestock losses to bears, or of the value of hunters, or of the fears or love of bears by hikers and cabin owners, than can a federal agency headquartered in Washington, D.C."

Historically the grizzly hunting season in Montana ran concurrently with the elk and deer seasons. During the two decades prior to the early 1970s when concerns were first raised about the grizzly's status in Montana, a fairly stable harvest of about 37 per year had occurred. As mentioned previously, a separate license for grizzly bear wasn't established until 1967.

In 1984 the season was set for Sept. 15 to Nov. 25 in the back-country hunting districts of the Bob Marshall Wilderness and surrounding areas and for Oct. 21 to Nov. 15 in most other districts open to grizzly hunjting. Of course, the subsequent early closure changed that because the quota limit for all kills was realized.

Basic grizzly requirements include that all grizzly licenses must be purchased by Aug. 31. Others are:

• There shall be no more than 25 grizzlies killed by hunting or any other human activity in the ecosystem generally referred to as the Bob Marshall ecosystem.

• The grizzly season will close on 48 hours notice in the 100 and 200 series districts when six female grizzlies have been killed by hunting or other human activity. This occurred in 1984.

• The grizzly season will close on 48 hours notice in the 400 series districts when three female grizzly bear have been killed by hunting or other human activity. This also occurred in 1984.

MOUNTAIN LION

Mountain lions became a game animal in Montana in 1971 and are now the object of two special seasons, one for hunting and another for chase only.

Relatively few hunters — only 1,000 licenses were sold in 1984 — go after lion, but those who do are both a dedicated and a hardy lot. The hunt characteristically involves the use of dogs and rigorous cross-country travel for many, many miles in mountainous terrain.

Not all lions live in the mountains, however. They are common throughout much of Montana, although the forested terrain in the western part of the state probably supports more of the secretive feline than other

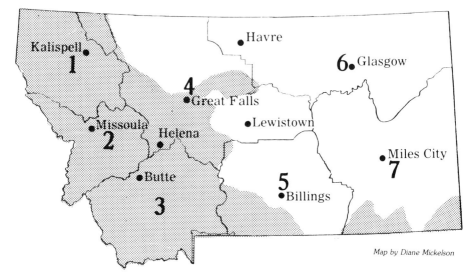

MOUNTAIN LION RANGE

Map by Diane Mickelson

habitats in the state. The Missouri Breaks country also is known to support a healthy mountain lion population.

Seasons vary from district to district each year. For example, in 1984 some ran from Sept. 15 through Feb. 15 and others from Dec. 1 through Feb. 15, while in one region the season was only from Jan. 1 to Feb. 15. Hunters are advised to check current regulations before going afield.

The limit is one adult mountain lion of either sex. Females with kittens may not be taken. It is recommended that if a lactating female is mistakenly killed, she should be backtracked and the kittens captured and turned over to the Department of Fish, Wildlife and Parks within 48 hours. Kittens are defined as the young of the year.

Evidence of sex must remain intact on the hide and no juveniles (with body spots) are to be killed.

A hunter killing a mountain lion is required to **personally** present the hide within 10 days to an officer of the Montana Department of Fish, Wildlife and Parks in the administrative region in which the license was filled, for the purpose of inspection, tagging and recording the kill.

A metal tag is attached to the hide upon inspection and must remain attached until the trophy is tanned. It is unlawful for anyone to possess, ship or transport any mountain lion, or part thereof, unless it has been tagged.

The chase season — in which no kills are made — requires only a free permit from the department, which is available in February. The chase season normally runs from mid-February to the end of April. Again, regulations as to the districts in which chase seasons are permitted vary from year-to-year and hunters are advised to check up-to-date regulations.

Chapter 7

Bird Hunting in Montana

By DON BURGESS

The Montana prairie wind was whooping it up across the rolling hill country near Shawmut. All of God's creatures were hiding out wherever the ridges or coulees tripped the wind and slowed it down a little. A high, gray cloud mass blocked the late fall sun, and the prairie itself looked forlorn, as if it would have liked a big coulee of its own to take shelter in.

From out of the west, like two dark stones plucked from the crest of the Crazy Mountains by the jet stream, hurtled a pair of birds, one a sage grouse, the other a large falcon. (Large, as falcons go, but still not as large as the sage grouse.) Across the gray sky they came, the grouse in the lead by about 20 yards, pumping its big, cupped wings, the falcon whipping the air with its twin scythe-blades bent back along its body like one of those Malmstrom Air Force Base Phantom jets. The gap between predator and prey — or between two powerful fliers just out there finding out which one was faster — neither narrowed nor widened as they passed over that piece of Sweetgrass County. An hour at that speed would've taken them both into North Dakota, and given the falcon an indelible memory of what the hind end of a sagehen looks like.

— — — — — — —

Something about that scene sticks in my mind as I look back over 30 years of bird hunting in Montana. Part of it might be sympathy with that big falcon; I'm pretty familiar with the hind ends of a lot of birds myself. They're not easy to catch up with sometimes, and once you get close, they can prove difficult to bring down.

Maybe it was the weather and the look of the land that day. It was rugged out there, and lonesome. Bird hunting in Montana can be like that, making you feel awfully insignificant, even foolish. Yet sometimes the best hunting is found on the days when normal people are snug in their easy chairs, watching TV and eating popcorn. And when you get into birds, in the sense of having a strong love of pursuing them, as well as in the literal sense of finding yourself surrounded by swarms of them, neither snow nor wind nor rain nor arctic air mass can quell the warmth within you.

I think the reason that isolated memory stands out for me, though, has more to do with the freedom of movement we enjoy in this big state, and with the freedom of movement that only the birds can know. The flight of all birds — and the high, determined flight of those two birds in particular — symbolized wildness and freedom and room-to-move. That falcon and that grouse are you and me and all the great, spirited, strong-hearted game birds that we yearn for, both as food for physical nourishment, and as something else not so easily defined.

Whenever we succeed in bringing down and holding in our hands a creature that's never recognized any political boundaries (other than maybe the fences around some of those little patches of country known as wildlife refuges) and is hardly bothered by any geographical bounds, for that matter, something happens — or should happen — inside us, something that goes beyond the need for food. We've overcome our own limits, in a sense, and come closer to the birds' world. Somehow, we've added something to ourselves.

Maybe that sounds a little perverse. But there just doesn't seem to be a totally satisfactory way of resolving the paradox inherent in killing creatures that we greatly admire. Every hunter has a little different way of saying it, if he or she talks about it at all. It's not easy to reckon just what is gained and what is lost when those perfect wings stop beating in mid-air, and that perfectly feathered body falls to the earth. For those who've heard the big cash register ring on lots of those sublime transactions, it has just somehow always been profitable. But dollars and cents really have nothing to do with it, and attempts to put the true value of it into words always fall short.

Teddy Roosevelt had his slant on it — the kind of view you might expect from a president: "Hunting breeds in men a sturdy self-reliance, for the lack of which in a nation, no other qualities can compensate." That sentence is a little hard to untangle, but to me it means, in part, that if you get out into the elements after the game, be it birds or four-legs, some of the vigor and spirit of those wild creatures is going to rub off on you. You'll wind up respecting them more, and understanding their needs better, too. (Which is what they need more than anything else to survive in this age.)

Excitement, exercise, "sturdy self-reliance", and maybe something nobody's figured out how to say yet. There's always something in bird hunting in Montana, whether we get our limit, or just get I ly to the comforts of home. All that beautiful country we've driven anu hiked and floated across makes every outing memorable. Knowing that if we couldn't find birds in one county today, we might find some six counties over tomorrow, is also something of value.

We can cross those county lines (recognizing that regulations change from area to area, and learning those regulations — that's part of the game) and fly for miles, like that falcon and that sagehen. There's a lifetime's worth of new country and new adventures out there. Sometimes the hardest part is just deciding where to start.

Waterfowl

It starts with the earth tipping its north pole away from the sun. A miniature ice age sets in every fall in the far north, and as the tundra lakes and ponds freeze up, clouds of web-footed, down-insulated birds fill the skies like feathers from a broken pillow, spiralling upward and shouting noisy farewells or "Let's get the flock out of here!" Then they spill southward, down across the mountains and prairies of Alberta and British Columbia and Saskatchewan, sailing in wide V's, bound for warmer climes.

The arrival of the "northern flight" is arguably the most magical, if not necessarily the most productive, part of waterfowling in Montana. The snow geese are usually in the lead, and their shrill voices stir the night as they come sailing across the country, awakening wild desires in hunter's hearts. Who can say what ancient wanderlust and subliminal sympathies and longings arouse us from our slumbers and move us outside into the cold October night air, still half asleep, to listen, to strain our eyes upward into the snow or fog to catch a glimpse of dim, vibrant forms; then to go and awaken the rest of the family, and call friends on the phone, and say, "Can you hear the snow geese? Go out and listen! The northern flight is on!"

If the weather is just right, and the geese need rest in that hour, and if you are in a town with street lights and there is a light snow or fog, you might go back outside and find those wild cries coming closer and closer, and see the white-winged wanderers illuminated by the lights of the town. Then you may forget where you are for a moment, and think of your gun and your shells, and make a move for the door. But then the magic may become too powerful for movement, and you stand still, and suddenly the geese are down on the ice of the street before your very eyes, or on your own glazed and shining lawn or roof, and you could no more shoot them than you could shoot Santa's reindeer.

The next morning there will be some vacant seats in the classrooms and offices around town. Out on the backroads, in the farm fields, around the reservoirs, and down along the river, the afflicted will search, or wait and watch, for the snows. There may be no second chance later in the season, for the snow geese come and go again like wraiths, with Mexico on their minds, and they might not stop in Montana at all, but for bad weather, or a little fatigue from covering maybe a thousand miles in the previous 48 hours.

Though they are seldom killed with any regularity by Montana hunters (except possibly around Freezeout Lake northwest of Great Falls, which is a fairly regular stopover point for those early migrants), the passage of the snow geese springs loose the waterfowler's passions with the promise that the rest of the northern host is on its way.

Sometime in October or November they'll arrive. Gradually, flock by flock, the northerns will descend on Montana grainfields, lakes, rivers and potholes. When you start seeing birds resting in places the local birds avoid, you can bet that they're migrants, unfamiliar with local customs. Just about every species of duck and goose native to North America will be represented, with the general exceptions of ocean ducks — scoters, old squaws, eider — and black ducks. Greater and lesser Canada geese, mallards, widgeon and pintails will predominate in numbers.

Drawn by the open water, some of the migrants will stick around until freeze-up, or until hunting pressure drives them on southward. Portions of the Missouri and Yellowstone rivers and their tributaries, along with isolated warm-water streams and sloughs, hold plenty of waterfowl in Montana through the season (which usually goes until around New Year's Day). Even along the frigid "Highline" between the North Dakota line and Cut Bank, a few spots — notably the roily waters below the spillways of Tiber Dam and Fort Peck Dam — stay open and hold birds well into the winter.

The creeks, ditches, and rivers of western Montana valleys tend to freeze over later than those of eastern Montana, and sometimes not at all. Large numbers of honkers and mallards will winter over in those areas; Pablo and Ninepipe National Wildlife Refuges in the lower Flathead Valley hold mallards right on through the early January closing dates. Even though the reservoirs usually freeze solid, the ducks remain, huddled in tight masses on the ice. Warm-water or spring-fed creeks in the area, along with the Flathead River, provide the necessary open water, and stubble fields provide the food. If the snow becomes too deep for them to forage in the stubble, they'll move south to the slightly more temperate Bitterroot Valley, congregating on the Lee Metcalf National Wildlife Refuge near Stevensville, and on the Bitterroot River channels and tributary creeks. Some will stop over on the lower Clark Fork River between Missoula and Frenchtown. A few will even linger in the high mountain valleys, from Clearwater Junction to Ovando and Deer Lodge. If the snow gets too deep they'll fly on out over the Bitterroot Range to try the

With mouth agape, a "honker," (Canada goose) lifts off a pond and lets the hunter know it doesn't like the intrusion.

valleys of Idaho and points south. A hardy few will always wait out the winter in Montana, settling for the insect and vegetable fare that the few areas of open, warm-water sloughs and creeks provide.

The determined waterfowler can find birds throughout the late-September to early-January season in Montana, even — sometimes especially — in cold weather. Ducks and geese get cold, too, and when they do, they're more reluctant to take to the air — preferring the 30 degree water to the -20 degree air. They're easier to decoy when it's cold and blizzarding out, and when jumped, they tend to hurry back to open water, sometimes circling right back to the same spot from which they arose.

When the last ice age pulled back, the glaciers rotted away gradually, until there were a lot of scattered blocks of thicker ice lying around on parts of what was to become the Montana prairies. The mud and gravel carried by the ice settled down on the ground surface around those remaining chunks as they melted away, leaving depressions filled with water. The ponds thus created are now known as "potholes." Today Montana's pothole country, in the northeast corner of the state and in the lower Flathead Valley, provides some of the most productive waterfowl breeding habitat on the continent, outside of Canada and Alaska.

Early in the hunting season, before the potholes have frozen over and all the locally-grown ducks have moved out, pothole country provides outstanding sport. You can hunt over decoys, either on the water or out in the grainfields, or find a small local "flyway" traveled by birds moving between ponds, or between ponds and grainfields, and just sit and pass-shoot from concealment. Or you can walk from pond to pond, attempting sneaks and surrounds, taking birds as they rise from the water.

"Local" ducks and geese (strictly the big Canadas) can also be found on farm ponds, stock reservoirs, lakes and streams all across Montana in the early season. After freeze-up, those that stick around will be congregated on whatever open water is left and on the refuges, along with some of the northerns. Finding them, early or late, is simply a matter of asking around at the corner gas station or sporting goods store, or driving around until you see them, and then obtaining permission to hunt, if they're on private land.

Public hunting areas, especially around the big refuges, occasionally become congested with hunters on opening days and holiday weekends. Tight regulations governing hunters' movements and positioning keep the situation from becoming chaotic. Hunters with the equipment and/or for-titude necessary for camping out at the gates the night before get the choice blinds, and are likely to get some fine shooting as the birds move back and forth to the feeding grounds in the morning. Competition for favored shooting blinds or pits under the birds' habitual flight paths has been known to cause fistfights. Disputes also arise sometimes over who shot which birds, as hunters race out to retrieve game. For those who eschew the restrictions on movement — and sometimes even on the number of shells that may be carried to the blinds — as well as the crowds, the competition, and the sky-busting, bird-crippling neophytes, there are still acres of private land. Not as much of it, especially in the heavy sub-divided western valleys, as there used to be, but enough to take some of the pressure off the public areas. The birds generally know where the refuges are, and that's where most of them will stay, but there are always a few flocks or pairs or singles hanging out in the countryside, even late in the season.

Finding the big refuges is easy. Finding the birds away from the refuges can be a little harder. It pays to spend time in the field, cruising country roads, hiking across farm fields to get to the creeks, or just taking up a good observation point wherever you think there might be birds. You'll eventually spot birds, and figure out their habits.

Waterfowling in Montana is a lot like the weather it hinges on: if you don't like the way things are going, wait a few minutes and they're likely to change. Ducks and geese have the most wonderful way of disappearing and appearing again. If you watch long enough, you'll be treated to some spectacles that can rival any outdoors experience anywhere for sheer power and excitement.

When 5,000 honkers rise off the ice at Pablo and head your way with the sound of a swarm of monster bees in a hurricane, you're liable to feel like the rest of the world just ceased to exist. When you get up a piney draw in the foothills of the Sapphires just before daylight and listen to flight after flight of mallards swooping into the grain from on high, sounding just like 747's about to touch down, you'll likely remember it for a while.

When you're at the end of a hundred-yard belly crawl up to the bank of the Missouri, and a group of honkers are suddenly launching themselves out from under you with deceptive speed, you're going to be filled with as much adrenalin as an infantryman in a firefight. Float the Bitterroot in a snowstorm, drift into the bank and crawl through the cottonwoods to a big backwater, try to pick one target out of the wall of big, robust, orange-legged northern mallards rising in front of you, and you'll be warm again, for sure.

The cottonwood tree dominates river and creek "bottoms" or riparian zones in Montana. Among the groves along the moving streams you may find wood ducks, teal, diving ducks (predominantly goldeneye and bufflehead), and Canada geese, as well as the ubiquitous mallard. Geese can surprise you anywhere at any time down among the cottonwoods, cruising silently at treetop level, or resting on broad gravel bars or riffles, or underneath cut banks.

A few Canadas have probably always nested in Montana, but only in the last 20 or 30 years have there been real huntable numbers of local geese. Wildlife managers have succeeded in creating suitable nesting habitat and sites on the national refuges, giving hunters a much better chance for taking geese throughout the season.

Prior to the establishment of the Lee Metcalf refuge in the Bitterroot Valley, for instance, there were no more than a dozen nesting pairs in the entire drainage from season to season. Now there are approximately 40 resident pairs, producing an average of 250 fledglings by fall. Where taking a goose once ranked right up there with taking a bull elk in order of difficulty, it is now more commonplace. The same successful program of habitat improvement has been going on even longer in the lower Flathead.

Whistling swans, nearly wiped out by the turn of the century, were protected in Montana for years. In 1974 they became fair game again, with 1,000 special permits currently available each year. These $2 permits are issued by drawings held in September. Applications are available from the Montana Department of Fish, Wildlife and Parks in Helena, and must be submitted in early September to the Special Licensing Division of FW&P. Permits are seldom sold out, especially in the Central Flyway portion of the state. (The dividing line between our two flyways, the Central and the Pacific, runs north and south along county lines, between Hill and Blaine counties in the north and Park and Carbon counties in the south.)

If you are interested in more meat for your money on a bird-for-bird basis, or in the thrill of bringing down one of these biggest American waterfowl, get a permit (limit: 1 per hunter per season) and go to Freezeout Lake, or Benton Lake, or Bowdoin, all in eastern Montana, in late October or early November. The swans, like the snowgeese, don't stay long, but when they arrive in those areas, they arrive in force, and provide some special thrills.

(Swan hunters should be mindful of the possibility of the endangered Trumpeter swans showing up in Montana. Though the few that are present here from time to time seldom use the same stopovers as the Whistlers, they're too valuable as individuals, and too vulnerable to extinction, as a species, to a mistake. About the only way to tell them from the whistlers is by their call. FW&P biologist Al Rossgaard of Havre likens this distinction to "the difference between a French horn and a flute." So if you're in doubt, don't shoot until you've heard the clear difference of their cries.)

At the other extreme, with the least meat for your money, bird-for-bird, are the snipe. Where do you find snipe? Oh, you know. Down there by the creek, where the cattle cross. Actually, these plump, quick little shore birds may flit up from under your nose almost anywhere in wet country, particularly, it seems, in cow pastures with a little moving water trickling through them.

It's rumored that snipe are tasty. It's a dim, weak rumor; snipe hunters, if they exist in Montana, are more secretive than the snipe are.

Snipe season begins in late September and ends after Christmas. The limit is usually around eight daily.

Upland Birds

Who was that man?
I'd like to shake his hand.
He made my day when he brought chinks to me.

Whoever it was who first brought Chinese pheasants to Montana sure put new words to an old song. If the sport of bird hunting was lacking anything here before 1895 (the reputed approximate date of their introduction), the presence of ringnecks has made up for it.

It wouldn't have been out-of-character for them to have come here on their own adventurous volition. Whether anybody actually carried them to Montana from somewhere else or not, I'm thankful for them. They were definitely doing well here by 1946, when I made the scene, and my dad brought them home for supper every fall that I can remember.

Those big cocks are almost as pretty coming out of the game pocket, all rumpled up, as they are when they launch out of the tules in splendid perfection. There's something as wonderful about seeing a pheasant — a bird with all the looks and style and speed of a Lamborghini or Alfa Romeo — as there is about eating one. It's practically unanimous that pheasant makes for some of the finest, most savory dining in the world. Whether the birds have grown up on rosehips, snowberries and grasshoppers, or on good old Montana wheat, pheasant is — pleasant.

From the Dakota border to the Bitterroots, from the Canadian line to the Yellowstone, the pheasant has done well, occupying every niche where some combination of wild rose, grain, cattails, Russian olives, elms, willows, cottonwoods, box elders, and sage grows. In short, you might find a pheasant just about anywhere you find farms.

The Lewistown area is well-known for its pheasants. So are the lower Flathead Valley, the Milk River bottoms and grainfields along the Highline, the Marias River area, and the Missouri and Yellowstone valleys. Good populations of pheasants range the wooded borders and sage flats near grainfields and other croplands just about anywhere in Montana.

Pheasants don't require grain, but where there is grain there'll be more birds than where there isn't. Corn, peas, beans, alfalfa, and sometimes beets and potatoes will also help a pheasant population along.

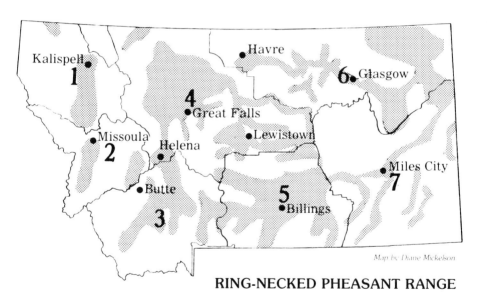

Map by Diane Mickelson

RING-NECKED PHEASANT RANGE

Pheasants thrive on variety in their habitat. If you see a piece of country in which the variety of vegetation types mimics the variety of colors in the cock's rainbow plumage, you'll likely find pheasants in it. Ringnecks behave in many ways like whitetail deer, and occupy much of the same habitat. Like whitetails, they are generally alert, wary, sneaky, hard-to-see, prolific, adaptable, and fond of farmlands. When hunting pressure gets hard, or when winter weather sets in, they'll yard up in the brush out of the wind, just like the deer. Pursuing them in harsh weather isn't easy on the hunter, but it can be most challenging, and often most profitable.

Early season hunts usually result in the heaviest game bags, until the younger, inexperienced birds are thinned out and the survivors made more wary. Mid- to late-season hunts may require more leg work, a good dog, and a willingness to beat the brush. A drive by one or two gunners through a brushy area, with maybe one or two others stationed at the far end, can produce some exciting shooting — along with scratched legs and cheeks, bruised shins, wads of burrs gluing your arms to your torso, and a good sweat. But when that old Missouri island bird with the 18-inch tailfeathers flashes and clatters and cackles up out of the brush and into the sunlight, followed by maybe 30 of his peers and progeny, it's pretty thrilling. Just hope you can get your gun barrel clear of the brush in time for a shot.

Pheasants raised at state-operated hatcheries at Warm Springs and two other sites used to be released in popular hunting areas around the state at the opening of the season. That program ended in 1982, with the advent and proven success of other state programs designed to improve and increase habitat. Private sportsmen's groups — notably the Ravalli County Fish and Wildlife Association — have also rebuilt wild populations through habitat improvement programs. Education and involvement of landowners in providing suitable cover and food plants for pheasants is improving the pheasant hunting in the Bitterroot Valley and other areas where residential development and "clean" agricultural practices (meaning "no weeds or brush allowed") have hurt birds and bird hunting.

The other Montana imports — Hungarian partridges (huns) and Chukar partridges — are as tasty as the Chinese pheasant, but not as colorful, or as numerous; and neither is much bigger in the body than a pigeon or a Cornish game hen.

Huns can be found just about anyplace you'll find pheasants, but they prefer more open country. They're seldom found in the kind of heavy, dense cover that pheasants prefer. They'll roost, as well as feed, out in the middle of stubblefields, dry pastures, or cropped-off hayfields; they also like dry hillsides with scattered bunchgrass and low sagebrush.

Chukars, which closely resemble Huns, are scarce in Montana, being less capable of surviving our winters. If you do run into some, in the two or three little areas of Montana where they've held their own, they'll probably be in dry, rocky, broken country. The presence of a grainfield or alfalfa crop in the vicinity of rugged hills and deep draws, in areas of very little precipitation, will help give Chukars a fair prospect of survival.

Montana's native upland birds are the mountain grouse, (ruffed, Franklins, and blue), the sharp-tailed grouse of the eastern and central prairies and foothills, and the sage grouse of eastern and southwestern sagebrush country.

Of all our game birds, these are the only ones that don't ordinarily get into the grainfields or other croplands, and are thus freer of possible pesticide contamination. It's a good feeling to take home a bird that you can cook and eat — skin, organs, fat and all — without worrying about poisoning yourself and your friends and family.

(Pesticide residues can turn up in almost any bird, however, so unless you are sure the one you're about to eat has spent all its life in a pristine wilderness or other relatively safe zone, discard the skin, fat and organs before cooking it, or at least before eating it.)

Grouse season usually opens in early September throughout most of Montana. It's a good time of year for combining berry-picking, picnicking, trout fishing, and a little big-game scouting with your hunts. When you get home with your birds, you can then combine some of the tastiest meat going with your fresh-from-the-woods fare, to start the fall off right.

Ruffed grouse, familiar to most U.S. hunters except those from the great plains and the southern third of the country, are common in western Montana's brushy mountain draws and bottomlands, and in the outlying ranges east of the Continental Divide. They can be found among the cottonwoods and willows along major streams, and from there right on up into blue grouse turf — the high ridges — when the grasshoppers are out.

Ruffeds love those pretty little low-elevation draws best,though, with their alder thickets and brook-trout streams and beaver ponds — the kinds of places that homesteaders fell in love with, logged off, grazed over, and went broke on. An early September hunt for ruffeds may lead you to one of those abandoned farmsteads with its ragged old apple orchards still turning out some delicious fruit.

Most of the best ruffed grouse habitat is on private land, or in the lower reaches of U.S. Forest Service and timber company land, so it's important to study maps and know the boundaries.

Blue grouse prefer the higher, drier reaches of mountainous country, east and west of the divide, especially after cool weather begins to wipe out the grasshoppers. Early in the season, though, large groups of blues may be found foraging in grassy areas adjacent to timber at lower elevations. By the time big game season comes around, they'll be way up there with the elk and mule deer, feeding on leaves and buds of certain low forbs and shrubs, and Douglas fir needles, eyes peeled for bobcats, goshawks and man. The young, inexperienced birds may sit around for a while and let you take aim, but the old and experienced will be up and away in a hurry, perching in the limbs, or shooting like sleek, gray missiles down across the draws. The challenge of negotiating the steep hills and high ridges of the timberlands makes blue grouse seldom cheap. In any case, their big, robust bodies make fine eating.

Franklin grouse, a type of spruce grouse, may show up just about anywhere there is dense coniferous forest (in the western quarter of the state, only). They're something like moose in their affinity for the dense timber, especially wet, sprucy, blowdown-ridden areas. They're also like moose in their propensity for turning up in unlikely places, including the lower elevation habitat of ruffeds and early-season blue grouse. There's also something moose-like about their seeming obliviousness to danger.

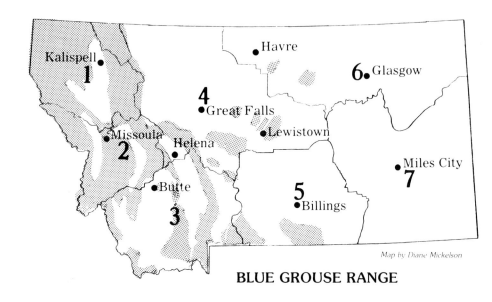

Map by Diane Mickelson

BLUE GROUSE RANGE

These birds, smaller and darker than blues, and lacking the top-knot and neck ruff of ruffeds, aren't nicknamed "foolhens" for nothing.

Many are taken with rocks, sticks, and air rifles. I've known them to fly up and land on my head, to sit still and let me prod them with sticks, and to attack wildly when I got too close to a brood of chicks. Such bravado is fitting in a moose, or even in smaller creatures that at least have sharp teeth or talons, but in a tender little grouse, it's plain foolishness.

I'm convinced that the only reason they still exist is that they will live in the kind of place other creatures usually avoid, such as cold, dark, blow-down jungles. From these secure seed-beds they are capable of sending out new stock every year to blunder around in the "real world" of coyotes and hawks and bobcats and men.

To give them the benefit of the doubt, it could be said that because they do tend to hang out in the dark reaches of the forest, they're just innocent, having encountered fewer people. Maybe ruffeds and blues used to be fools, too, before people started tramping up every creek and ridge, with a craving for gold and a taste for wild chicken. The young of ruffeds and blues can also be taken with rocks, sticks and air rifles now and then, but they will at least act a little nervous when approached. If you find yourself in a covey of Franklins, leave some for seed. Coming home with a limit of Franklins is nothing to brag about, especially if they all came from the same patch of forest.

All of the mountain grouse have a weakness for the fine gravel found on road beds, and many are taken early in the season by hunters driving

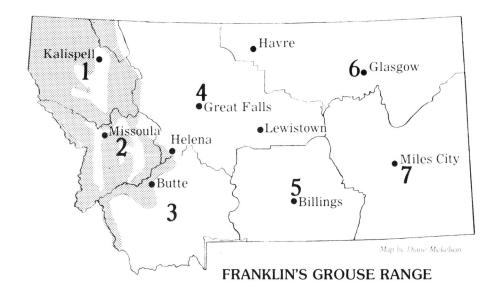

FRANKLIN'S GROUSE RANGE

mountain roads early or late in the day. It's a good way to get meat, but it doesn't produce many of the other benefits of sport hunting.

Sharptails are another strange bird. Strange, anyway, to hunters accustomed to mountain and woodland grouse, and new to the prairie. Maybe it's the wide-open spaces that inspire sharptails to fly high in the sky like runt eagles, clucking their guttural, staccato, chicken-like clucks. Maybe it's the lack of trees that causes them to squat happily, pigeon-like, on phone lines, barbed-wire fence strands, or the roof-ridges of abandoned honyocker cabins.

And maybe it's the lonesomeness of wild, barren hills and prairie that makes this beige and white bird, with a tail like a female pintail duck, get together in the early fall with 20 or 30 or 40 of its neighbors, as if for a hoedown. Then again, maybe they figure there's some kind of safety in numbers, in a land patrolled by fierce raptors. Goshawks, golden eagles, falcons, red-tailed and rough-legged hawks, and great horned owls take every opportunity to nab the tasty, dark-fleshed sharptail. Maybe these grouse like the feel of the odds, when banded together — though the raptors might pick off any number of them, there are still lots of them to keep each other company.

Whatever their reasons, sharptails do band up, and if you chance upon a large group in dense cover — a patch of chokecherry or buffalo or wild roses in some semi-moist crease in the prairie — they may oblige you by taking off one at a time, or by twos and threes, so that you can pick them off like clay pigeons coming out of a trap, until you have your five- or six-bird limit; or you can miss your first shots and still have time to reload.

But then again, the whole squadron may sally forth as one bird before you get into range, and be gone clucking into the next county, leaving you standing out in the middle of a section of territory whose entire population of sharptails has just left.

Sharptails hang out on windswept ridges or knolls in cold weather and snow, especially if the sun is out and there are some exposed, sun-warmed rocks to snuggle beside or stand on. Isolated patches of brush and any kind of cover around the edges of hayfields or stubble are liable to shelter birds. In the drylands, every little seep or stock-tank may draw birds during the day. If there's a stream or pothole in the area, it may pay to have some #4 shot shells ready, in case some ducks make themselves available. Don't be surprised, either, if you kick up some Huns or ringnecks while you're at it.

Part of the great beauty of the eastern two-thirds of Montana is the surprising variety of game you may encounter in a given locale. If you study your regulations and time your outing right, you could wind up with a very mixed bag.

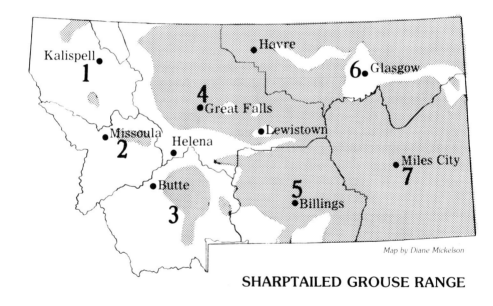

Map by Diane Mickelson

SHARPTAILED GROUSE RANGE

Sagehen. Sage Grouse.

"Cock of the Plains" is what Lewis and Clark called this largest of North American grouse. Interesting birds, these, especially the first time you stumble into a bunch of them and they go flapping off like a flock of big, cupped-wing owls. Once considered the most abundant bird in the west,

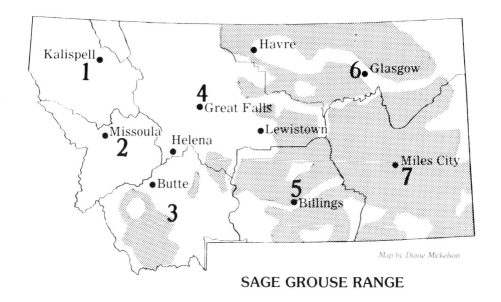

SAGE GROUSE RANGE

Map by Diane Mickelson

sagehens went into drastic population declines when the prairies were grazed heavily by livestock in the early 1900s. They're still numerous in Idaho, Wyoming and Montana, however, and in Montana there are still around 11 million acres of the kind of sagebrush-grassland country that's critical to their survival.

But sagehen country is the same kind of undernourished, underwatered, underdeveloped country that the men looking for nuclear waste dump sites like, and there's coal under a lot of it, and farmers are always looking for ways to get rid of sagebrush. Those kinds of interests can see to the destruction of a lot of habitat in a hurry. Sagehens are sensitive, despite their apparent size and vigor. They just don't make it in anything but that desolate sage country that only they — and antelope and jackrabbits and cowboys — can really love.

Actually, sage grouse enjoy alfalfa and other leafy vegetation, but come fall they leave it all behind in favor of sage leaves. Out in that thin-soiled, prickly pear-ridden, wind-blown semi-desert, the big cocks and hens stroll with quiet deliberateness, one eye out for eagles, and the other out for coyotes, pecking off the little, silver-gray sage leaves with delicate precision, with a bill big enough to split walnuts. And in a country so loaded with grit and gravel of the kind other birds will brave freeway traffic to get, the sagehens don't take any of it. They only eat leaves and insects which need no grinding.

Sagebrush never having enjoyed quite the favor among humans that true sage has as a flavor-enhancer (you know sagebrush isn't a true sage, but that's what it's called by almost everybody who doesn't have a Ph.D. in botany) it is not surprising that a creature which consumes so much of it, especially during hunting season, is not highly regarded as table fare. Sagehen meat is dark, purplish, lean and somewhat coarse, like that of a wild goose. Though the flavor is not particularly reminiscent of sagebrush, there's something about sagehen that makes you tend to grab another package of mule deeer burger instead of the one labeled "sagehen" when you go to the freezer. It's not bad, really, just not preferred by anybody I know. But I haven't a doubt in the world that there's somebody out there with a recipe for it that would change our preferences.

Meanwhile, the species doesn't stand in danger of being killed off due to culinary demand. Coal mining, uranium processing, agricultural encroachment, maybe. Hunting, no.

Seasons on all Montana grouse run well into big game seasons in many areas, setting up the possibility of combination hunts on almost any outing. The trouble is, of course, when you decide to carry the shotgun you run into big game, and when you're carrying your rifle you're sure to run into grouse. Decision, decisions.

Turkey

Thirteen wild Merriam's turkeys from Colorado were brought into Montana and planted in the Judith Mountains in 1954. The state biologists who brought them went back for 44 more over the next three years and turned them loose in central and southeastern Montana. Those first plants reproduced successfully, and soon their progeny were being trapped and transplanted to other parts of the state, where they're doing well enough that over 1,000 of them are now being harvested annually by hunters.

Out in certain areas of dry, piney hills and flats, from Eureka to Glasgow, and from Darby to Miles City, this state has turkeys. And they've received a lot of admiration from the adventurous, pioneer, Montana turkey hunters, who've put in for permits and gone out — without benefit of any passed-on-from-father-to-son-know-how — and found turkeys where there never before was such a creature.

In fact, turkey hunting has taken on a mystique akin to that of elk hunting, especially during the April hunts for breeding toms. In the spring, the tom turkey goes on the prod something like a bull elk does in the fall, with big, old birds taking harems of hens and gobbling every bit as lustily as a breeding bull elk bugles. The toms can be called in by using a variety of devices to imitate their gobbles and "yelps" of hens.

In the fall season the young of the year are available, and both hens and toms may be taken.

Expert turkey caller Rob Hazlewood of Helena poses with a turkey he took in northcentral Montana. Hazlewood is a founder of the Cedar Hill Game Call Co. and has been a leader in the adaptation of the diaphragm call for use in elk calling.

Turkeys are exceptionally alert, vigorous, cautious birds, possessed of extremely good eyesight. They've been known to exit quickly upon seeing a man's eyelid fall and rise in what is known as a blink. Gone in the blink of an eye, so to speak.

Dawn finds a flock of turkeys roosting in the tops of these pine trees in northcentral Montana. Turkey have steadily increased in popularity as their numbers have increased and seasons were established in several areas in the state.

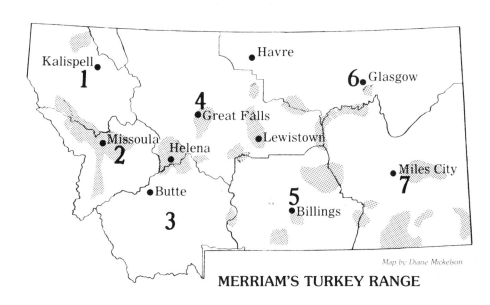

Map by Diane Mickelson

MERRIAM'S TURKEY RANGE

When they go, they're a blur of power and speed, flying like a big copper kettle with a rocket engine, or running like a giant pheasant, taking two-yard strides and hitting 25 m.p.h. on straightaways. Their feathers are thick and tough, and the 20-pound toms sport a mass of fatty tissue, called a breast sponge, on their chests, making them difficult to bring down. Their ability to take shot (could it be fairly said that they take more killing, pound for pound, than a Cape Buffalo?) coupled with their speed and wariness, wins them plenty of respect, and makes addicts (and sometimes fools) out of those who pursue them. If they only sported some kind of antlers, there's be a turkey camp and outfitter and guide ser vices in about 30 more Montana counties by now.

Doves

The newest entree on the Montana hunters' menu is a little bird that's been here all along. But prior to 1984, the only people who hunted Montana-born-and-raised mourning doves were Texans and Mexicans, and people who went to Texas and Mexico to hunt them. If a Montanan wanted to shoot doves legally, even if they'd been raised on his own grain crop, he had to follow the birds 2,000 miles south in September or October, and buy a nonresident's license.

Now we have a two-month dove season that begins in early September, with a daily bag limit of 15 birds. Most doves have flown south by the early-November season closure, but a few isolated flocks may be found wintering in-state.

Who knows why it took so long to get a dove season in Montana? Maybe the Texans hired Helena lobbyists to protect the free flow of doves southward. Maybe Montanans figured that a dinky little bird like that wasn't worth shooting at, and just let those hard-up Texans have them. And maybe, too, it took a long time to overcome landowners' concerns for additional hunting pressure on much of the land where doves are found.

Anyway, dove shooting is here. The tally isn't in yet on how well received doves were in their first year as legal targets, but chances are there were a few Texas-transplant hunters afield in Montana, taking up their old sport again. It's just a matter of time before their bragging will aggravate some Montanans into sneaking out to try their hand at bringing down some of those little gray featherballs.

The annual dove crop springs up all across Montana, wherever stands of trees or brush suitable for nests and roosts are situated near grain and water. Doves are prolific, even though they normally raise just two young per nest. They're the most widespread of the 10 dove species found in the western U.S. (the only other species found in Montana is the rock dove, or common pigeon). By September the young doves look just about like their parents, and can fly just about as fast; then they'll begin flocking into

Montana grainfields by the hundreds.

Like the water that runs out of Montana's mountains, bound for downstream states, Montana's doves are soon ready to head across the border. We've reserved the use of some of that flow in-state now, but with doves being as hard to hit as the articles in the sporting journals say they are, the dove season in Montana isn't going to make much difference to those downstream users. At least not for a few years yet — not until Montana hunters also realize that dove hunting is also as exciting a shooting sport as those same sporting journals say it is.

— — — — — — — —

With millions of acres to hunt on under the Big Sky, and millions of birds to chase, we Montana bird hunters have our work cut out for us just finding time to see and do it all.

It's out there to be enjoyed — to freeze, frustrate and fool us, to drain our gas tanks and our personal energy reserves, to fill our freezers with meat and our hearts with song, and maybe even to give us some of that good old "sturdy self-reliance."

It comes down to picking out a species to pursue, and a piece of country in which to do it, and then trying to narrow the gap down to without about 40 yards and, finally, making a good shot and a good retrieve.

Easier said than done, sometimes. Ask any falcon.

Don Burgess is a Montana native and a lifelong hunter. He was raised in Missoula and also has lived in Helena and Havre so he's familiar with the state's incredible variety in bird habitat and hunting. He currently works as a school teacher on the Rocky Boy Reservation near Havre.

Chapter 8

Bighorn Sheep
Mountain Goat - Moose

There are several "trophy" species that require special permits issued by drawings in Montana: bighorn sheep, mountain goat and moose. In each case the competition is intense for the limited number of permits available.

And yet the odds of getting a permit have remained fairly stable in recent years — staying at a 3 percent success rate for those wanting moose, 6 percent for mountain goat and an average of 12 percent for bighorn sheep. What hasn't remained constant is the cost of a permit. They've more than doubled in the past decade, raising the question of whether the average hunter hasn't been literally priced out of the market. Some of the permits now cost several hundred percent of what they did in 1970.

For example, from 1970 to 1984 the individual moose and bighorn sheep permits went from $25 to $52 for residents and from $50 to $302 for nonresidents. Permits to hunt goats went from $15 to $52 for residents and from $30 to $302, and bighorn sheep from $25 to $52 for residents and from $50 to $302 for nonresidents.

Proponents of such increases insist, probably correctly, that many hunters are willing to pay these prices for the chance to hunt and take a trophy and that permit fees add needed funds to the coffers of the Montana Department of Fish, Wildlife and Parks. Such arguments miss the mark, however. The higher rates have literally served to make hunting these trophy animals a privilege for the wealthy or at least the well-to-do. Because of economic conditions they can't control, many sportsmen are deprived of a fair chance at enjoying a public hunting resource.

My letter file and phone records indicate major dissatisfaction with these high permit fees among average sportsmen. I personally think it is a tragedy that the fees have grown too high for the average person, particularly in the case of moose, where the object of the hunt is more often to obtain meat rather than to garner a mountable trophy. I agree with the sentiments of one irate, long-time Montana hunter who called in 1984 to complain that it appeared to him that state management personnel were more interested in making big bucks on the trophy animals than they were in protecting the interests of average sportsmen.

Nevertheless, managing each of these species in a way that will allow them to be maintained on the list of species that can be hunted is strongly in the interests of all hunters. It is important for hunters to keep the battle over fairness in the marketplace separate from that concerning management and habitat issues. Otherwise, we'll be back to the good old days of not being able to hunt anything. It is a fact that both moose and bighorn sheep have made remarkable recoveries over the last 40 years.

MOOSE

Even though it is the largest native game animal found in Montana, the moose has never played a major role in hunting circles — except as a prized "extra" for both the trophy and meat hunter.

Moose are largely confined to southwestern, western and northwestern Montana. In 1984 a total of 682 permits were issued in 63 hunting districts. Your chances of drawing a permit were approximately 1 in 80, but those who did get permits were, as is usually the case, extremely successful. Between 70 and 90 percent of those who get permits take a moose most years, although the success rate has dipped as low as 54 percent.

The Shiras Moose found in Montana (*Alces alces shirasi*) is a distinct subspecies of the Rocky Mountain moose and compared to other moose populations is both smaller and paler in coloration. This subspecies, named by the late Dr. Edward W. Nelson, chief of the U.S. Biological Survey (forerunner of the U.S. Fish and Wildlife Service) in honor of George Shiras III, a naturalist who documented the subspecies' existence, is found not only in Montana but also throughout the mountains of Idaho, Wyoming, Utah, occasionally Colorado, southwest Alberta and southeast British Columbia.

Even if the Shiras is a smaller subspecies, this Montana moose is monstrous — a bull will stand six feet or more at the shoulders and weigh as much as 1,200-1,400 pounds. Cows are smaller, usually weighing 600-800 pounds. The bulls have extremely large antlers and because they are palmated, they appear even more massive than they really area. Consequently, the moose is an imposing figure wherever found — usually isolated in a high, wet mountain basin or in thickly-forested bottomland along streams or in moist meadow sites or in and around beaver ponds.

"For years, it was popularly believed that moose were restricted to

Bruce Todd of Trego, Montana, took this trophy moose in the northwestern part of the state. Its 171 and 7/8ths points placed it tenth on the Boone and Crockett record list for Montana.

valley bottoms and limited to a diet of willows and aquatic vegetation," according to Mike Aderhold of the Montana Department of Fish, Wildlife and Parks. "This after all was where the animal was most accessible and easily observed and most often photographed."

But research has shown that most moose migrate from low elevation winter ranges to higher elevations in the summer and early fall, Aderhold noted. A few moose, however, seem to be year-around residents at both high and low elevations. This certainly jibes with what I've encountered over the past 30 years. I grew up in the excellent "moose country" of northwestern Montana and often during hikes, summer and winter, I encountered moose in the high basins of the upper Whitefish Range. Later, after my outdoors activities shifted to the higher, more open mountains of southwestern Montana near Dillon, I found the same thing: moose stayed in deep snow in the high basins. But overall, most of the moose I've encountered over the years have been in the stream bottoms.

Moose have been observed eating several dozen plants, but most of their diet is the stems of evergreen and deciduous shrubs and trees. D.R. Stevens, writing in the book *Game Management in Montana*, noted that moose adapt their food habits to browse available in various habitat types. At higher elevations, low huckleberry, willow and subalpine fir are most important. At lower elevations, Douglas-fir, dogwood, serviceberry and chokecherry may form the bulk of the diet and, where available, willow is important to moose.

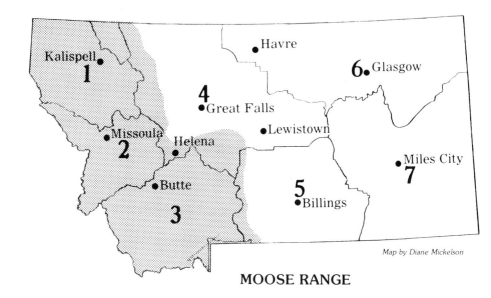

Map by Diane Mickelson

MOOSE RANGE

The first recorded sighting of moose occurred along the Missouri River on May 10, 1805, in the vicinity of the Milk River when John Ordway, a member of the Lewis and Clark Expedition, recorded in his journal that the party "Saw mooce deer which was much larger than the common deer." Meriwether Lewis noted the first actual shooting of a moose on July 7, 1806, along the Blackfoot River in the vicinity of the present town of Lincoln: "Reuben Fields wounded a moos deer this morning near our camp."

Hunting for moose in Montana is a far cry today from what it has been throughout most of the state's history. Moose hunting was closed in the state in 1897 when it was believed that the species was extinct in the state. Then at the turn of the century, George Shiras documented the species' existence in the Yellowstone. Although moose hunting wouldn't legally occur again until 1945, it was realized that moose still existed throughout the isolated mountain basins and along undeveloped stream channels.

The half-century-long closure of moose hunting enabled careful documentation not only of the moose's widespread distribution throughout western Montana, but also its adaptability to changing habitat conditions. When moose hunting finally resumed, it was obvious that their numbers were substantial enough to permit rigid population control measures. While over the years some increase has been realized in the number of moose taken annually, moose populations have remained fairly stable.

During that first season in 1945, 90 permits were issued — 40 in the Absaroka, 30 in the Gallatin and 20 in the Big Hole. By 1969 the number of permits issued had increased to 668 for all of southcentral and western Montana. Four hundred and fifty-seven moose were harvested that year.

In 1983, 581 permits were issued and 481 moose killed, a success rate of 85 percent.

Moose hunting is rigidly controlled district-by-district with the season running from Sept. 15 to the end of the general hunting season. Quotas are set for each district, some for either-sex and some for antlered bulls only. Hunters are advised to check the hunting maps carefully each year. District quotas change each year. You might find that one year you can hunt either cows or bulls in a certain district while the next year that district is limited to antlered bulls only.

This system of quotas results in the issuance of 550-600 permits each year, yielding a sustainable harvest of about 500 moose.

Of major importance to wildlife managers is the fact that most critical moose habitat in Montana is on public land, particularly that managed by the U.S. Forest Service. In the past, some habitat manipulation to improve livestock forage on public lands has been detrimental to moose populations. According to research done by the Department of Fish, Wildlife and Parks, key moose forage has been heavily impacted through the removal of brush to increase grass forage for commercial livestock and the use of herbicides to improve forage for livestock, while damaging forage for moose.

Forest roading is another problem. Research is now underway in northwestern Montana where key moose habitats on the Kootenai, Flathead and Lolo National Forests will undoubtedly be impacted by forest plans to more than double their road system and increase timber harvests. These studies, which began in 1981, hopefully will provide the information to determine what moose need to survive. For example, it is hoped that officials will be able to coordinate the timing, spacing and methods of logging with the needs of local moose populations.

MOUNTAIN GOAT

One of the most sought-after and prized big game trophies in Montana is the mountain goat. It also is one that requires considerable commitment to hunt, particularly if the lucky permit holder hasn't taken his or her trophy by the time deep mountain snows come to the difficult terrain where most goats are found.

From 170 to 230 goats are taken each year in Montana, despite the fact that seasons have been tightened up in recent years. Goats are fairly easy to locate, not only because their white coats make them stand out on rocky mountainsides, but because they're fairly limited in the type of terrain they choose to live in. Thus, it isn't too difficult for the hunter to put himself in good goat country — particularly if preseason scouting has been done.

What is difficult is to move about in that country and take a nice trophy. Goats inhabit rugged terrain. Most of their range is between 5,000 to 11,000 feet and particularly during the early part of the season, which

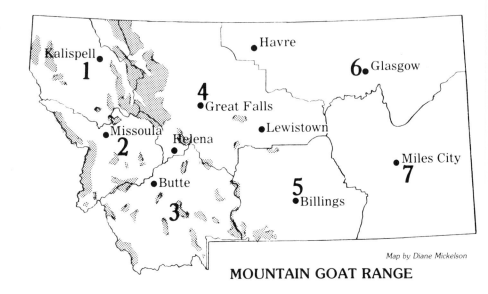

Map by Diane Mickelson

MOUNTAIN GOAT RANGE

traditionally runs from Sept. 15 to the close of general hunting season, they're isolated at the highest extremes of their range.

Goats tend to use the higher parts of their range in the summer and move to lower elevations for winter, but some observers have reported just the opposite to be true for some populations. They move to higher elevations in the winter to forage on slopes exposed by wind.

Mountain goats (*Oreamnos americana missoulae*) are unique. There isn't another animal like them in the world. They've awed viewers with their incredible agility on steep rock faces ever since the first sightings of them — Capt. James Cook labeled them "white bears" when he saw them for the first time in British Columbia in the 1700s.

Throughout their recorded history, mountain goats have been misidentified as sheep, white antelope, white bear and possibly other things. Arnold Foss and Merle Rognrud, writing for the Montana Department of Fish, Wildlife and Park's book *Game Animals of Montana,* noted that old records of goat sightings have to be interpreted with care because it was common to misidentify them.

"Early authorities considered the goat a hunter's myth rather than a creature of reality," they wrote. "The journals of Lewis and Clark had few entries concerning goats. Members of the expedition of Alexander Ross in 1823 and 1824 saw numerous goats in the Bitterroot Valley."

The Bitterroot is still excellent goat country, but goats are found throughout most of Montana's mountainous terrain. Permits were issued for 44 districts in 1984, with the most, 75, being in the Bitterroot. Other drawing quotas were for as few as two or three to a district to highs of 25 in the Absaroka area, 20 in the South Fork of the Flathead and 20 in the Bitterroot's West Fork drainage. Quotas in most districts have been reduc-

Jack Atcheson Sr. of Butte with a 10-inch billy taken in late November 1983 in the Bitter-root Mountains. Atcheson is one of Montana's most widely-known hunting authorities and earned a worldwide reputation as a taxidermist before becoming a hunting consultant more than 30 years ago.

ed in recent years and it appears that trend will continue as goat management is refined.

Because goats live at high elevations, vegetative growth is hindered by short growing seasons and cool temperatures and a generally difficult environment — cliffs and steep, rocky hillsides don't produce a lot of forage. Goats use grass and grass-like plants throughout the year, but depend most heavily on them in fall and winter. Forbs are their most important summer food.

Goat hunting has had a spotty history in Montana. The first official season was established in 1905 when the hunter was restricted to one goat per hunting season. This lasted for several years and then the entire state was closed to the hunting of goats. From 1929 to 1935, a season was authorized for goats on the west side of the Bitterroot River in Ravalli County, but 1936-38 saw a closure in effect throughout the state.

Parts of Flathead, Lewis and Clark, Missoula, Powell and Ravalli Counties were open to goat hunting in 1939 and 1940. From 1941 to 1950 areas open to goat hunting varied greatly from one year to the next. In 1951 goat hunting was open only in the upper South Fork of the Flathead River and during 1952 and 1953 the upper Middle Fork of the Flathead and Spotted Bear River drainages were included for a five-day period.

A special goat license was created in 1953 in an attempt to control the number of hunters in a given area, but it wasn't until 1971 that several unlimited goat districts were eliminated and goat hunting went strictly to a

Photo courtesy Montana Department Fish, Wildlife & Parks

Transportation was accomplished whatever way was necessary during the early goat transplant program. In the photo above, Jim McLucas is shown taking mountain goats on a pack animal to make a transplant.

drawing process for all districts in the state where goat hunting is permitted.

A major factor enabling the increase in goat hunting during this period was a vigorously pursued transplant program. From 1961 to 1969, officials trapped and transplanted 228 goats from native and established herds and released them in new areas. Hunting seasons were not opened until 10 to 15 years after the transplants, but the transplant program did substantially increase hunting recreation in Montana. Of the 650 limited goat permits issued in 1965, 190 or 29 percent were for hunting areas where goats did not exist prior to the transplant program.

Hunters now are required to present, or contact for presentation, to MDFWP officials the complete head with horns attached or the top portion of the skull with horns attached within 10 days of the date of kill. This way, more and more biological data is collected to continue refinement of the management process.

Should you draw a permit, the following recommendations may improve your chances for success:

1. Familiarize yourself with the area you intend to hunt. A fishing trip to a high mountain lake in the area before hunting season may serve this purpose. Get good maps and information from local wildlife and land management agencies.

2. Plan to hunt early in the season. Most goats are killed then when the weather is milder and lack of snow makes the goats easier to see and

facilitates your travel.

3. Be in condition for strenuous exertion at high altitudes. This will minimize your chances of accident or illness and increase your chances to take a goat.

4. Be prepared for a variety of weather conditions. Everything from warm Indian summer days to raging blizzards may occur.

5. Plan to stay for several days if possible. Hunters who stay for five or more days have better hunting success than a week-end hunter.

6. Wear suitable footgear. Sturdy, rubber-soled boots should be worn for comfort and safety when hiking in the steep, rocky areas frequented by goats.

7. Pack a generous length of rope with your hunting equipment. It may get you out of a tight spot on a cliff and can be used to lower your trophy down a steep slope or a cliff.

8. Use efficient hunting methods. A good technique is to walk to a good observation point and scan the surrounding cliffs and peaks with binoculars to locate the quarry. Then a careful stalk will usually bring you within shooting distance.

9. If you are after a big billy, he can usually be recognized because he is alone and has a buffalo-like hump on his shoulders. A nanny will often have long horns, but the horns are not as heavy as a billy's.

10. Place your shot carefully. Unless dropped in its tracks, a goat may crawl or fall onto an inaccessible ledge and die, or roll down the mountain and break its horns or ruin its hide.

BIGHORN SHEEP

No big game trophy is more emotionally pursued than the bighorn sheep ram. Small wonder, too! With its massive, sweeping horns, it is one of the most beautiful of trophies and its meat is as prized now as throughout its recorded history in Montana.

These qualities have always made the bighorn (*Ovis Canadensis canadensis*) a cherished trophy, but its preference for fairly open country and need for habitat that just happens to also serve its domestic counterpart has made it susceptible to decimation.

For most of the period of recorded history in Montana, the bighorn faced death and decline. Then, in 1941, a turnaround occurred. Scientific management principles brought on by passage of the Pittman-Robertson Act laid the groundwork for hunters' money to finance one of the most remarkable big game recoveries in history. Not only was the bighorn brought back in many areas, it now is providing hunting opportunities in more than 20 districts in widely separated parts of Montana. Montana's herd is estimated at 3,500.

In 1983, the last year for which statistics are available, 316 bighorns were taken by 351 hunters. This represented a stable harvest at incredibly

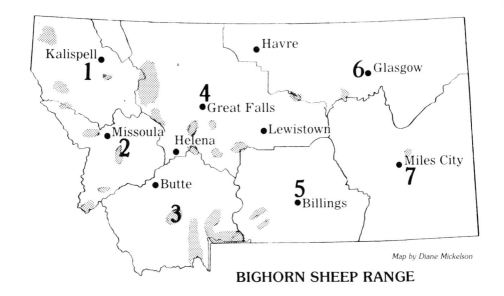

Map by Diane Mickelson

BIGHORN SHEEP RANGE

high levels, especially since the harvest hadn't even reached 200 in any previous year and didn't top 100 until 1981.

Bighorn sheep were plentiful in Montana at the time Lewis and Clark first recorded their presence. They were still plentiful throughout much of the state's early history, at least through the trapping and early settlement days. No official estimate is available on how many bighorns there were in Montana, but approximately 2 million existed in North America. Early records from a variety of sources document that sheep were found in portions of the mountainous country from the Montana-Wyoming border all the way to the mountains of Idaho in western Montana. In addition, bighorn populations also were recorded in many of the isolated mountain regions of Montana, the Bearpaw, Big Belt, Crazy, Highwood, Bull and Judith mountains.

Three factors contributed to the decline in bighorn sheep — competition with domestic livestock for range, diseases contracted from domestic sheep, and hunting.

Of these, the most serious has been diseases contacted from domestic sheep. The bighorn historically has been the loser in these contacts, which begin with range competition and overuse followed by malnutrition and subsequent death from such diseases as scabies, anthrax, lungworm and pneumonia-like disease.

The Sun River herd was decimated in the winter of 1925 and similar die-offs occurred there in 1927 and 1932. Other herds to suffer included the Rock Creek and Stillwater herds and another herd in Glacier National Park where numbers plummeted from 1,500 in 1916 to an estimated 165 in 1967.

Most of the hunting impact on bighorns took place in the years leading to a historic turning point in bighorn history in Montana — the kill of the last known Audubon bighorn, a subspecies of sheep that had adapted to living in the dry and rugged breaks country along the Missouri River in northcentral Montana. That incident occurred in the Billy Creek area of the breaks and has been seen since as a benchmark of tragic proportions.

But it would take more than the historic demise of a subspecies even as admired as the Audubon bighorn to turn things around for the mountain bighorns. By 1930, wild sheep in Montana were reduced to small remnant bands that were unhealthy, unproductive and considered by many to be an endangered species. And by 1941, they were at a low ebb both in density and distribution. The stage had been set for the hunter and wildlife manager to undertake the bighorn comeback.

Research began hand-in-hand with management programs as soon as money became available in 1941 under the Pittman-Robertson wildlife restoration funds. Transplantings and improved habitat conditions for bighorn sheep combined to facilitate marked improvements in bighorn numbers. There now are 11 major herds in Montana and 13 other areas have been restocked by transplanting with variable results.

Among the improvements are acquisition of the Sun River Game Range, which allowed elk to move out of the mountainous winter range to the foothills, taking considerable pressure off bighorn range. Marked reductions in domestic sheep competition for vital forage on national forest lands also has helped and in some critical areas bighorns have benefitted from reductions of other big game animals.

The Sun River herd is a marvelous success story. Following the massive die-offs in the late 1920s and early 1930s, only 159 bighorns could be located there. Their population level remained static and research showed they were suffering from competition with elk, deer and domestic livestock. Then the Sun River Game Range acquisition led to large increases in that specific bighorn herd. By 1974-75 the herd had increased more than 500 percent to 900 bighorns.

In addition, less spectacular increases took place in the West Rosebud Creek, Spanish Peaks and Stillwater herds.

The transplant program that succeeded so well in helping bring the bighorn sheep back in Montana has taken on legendary proportions. Over the years more than 1,000 bighorns have been trapped and transplanted in Montana, with transplants made in 27 areas. About 10 new herds have been established and seven transplant attempts have proven unsuccessful.

One of the principal participants in that drama was Jim McLucas of the Montana Department of Fish, Wildlife and Parks, who now is retired and long has been one of my heroes in the saga of wildlife management in Montana. Here's a comment he made about the transplants in 1981:

"The use of helicopters has certainly simplified the job of getting sheep from one place to another. There were some real logistical problems

Photo courtesy Montana Department Fish, Wildlife & Parks

Transplanting bighorn sheep and mountain goats under the technology of the time required the use of mules and horses in some places. Transplants were a major factor in the resurgence of bighorn sheep in Montana.

when we started trapping programs in the early 1940s. It took lots of sweat and time then, even though sheep are relatively docile animals to handle. I can recall walking rams down the mountain with a lariat over each horn. On other occasions the regal animals suffered (the) indignities of bumpy wheelbarrow rides. Horses packed with sheep in wooden crates was another method of transportation."

The transplanting programs began in the spring of 1942 when two rams and nine ewes were trapped in the Sun River Canyon and transplanted to the Gates of the Mountains area near Helena. Another ram and two ewes were released the following year.

That first transplant failed. The sheep scattered and were never seen again; subsequent transplants would see sheep enclosed until they became accustomed to an area.

In 1947, three rams and four ewes from the Sun River area were released on Wildhorse Island in Flathead Lake. They joined with four ewes already on the island, which had been brought in as lambs from Cranbrook, British Columbia. The Wildhorse sheep were of major importance to the success of sheep transplanting in Montana — bighorns from that herd were destined to eventually provide the nucleus for several other sheep herds in the state.

McLucas also related one of the most disappointing attempts at establishing a herd of sheep in the historical sheep range along the

One of Montana's most successful trophy hunters, Arlie Burk of Eureka poses with a fine bighorn ram taken in Lincoln County. It was the second excellent ram he has taken from this general area over the years.

Missouri River above Fort Peck Reservoir. Montana traded with the Colorado Fish and Game Department for five rams and 11 ewe bighorns. They were released in 1947 into a large fenced area in the Missouri Breaks on the hope that after spending several years within a fenced area, the sheep would consider the breaks home.

It didn't work. After holding the sheep for several years and allowing natural propagation to expand the herd's size to about 100, the fences were taken down. There even were a few hunting seasons conducted for 3/4-curl rams in the breaks, but the sheep gradually dispersed and faded away. Some were seen as far as 50 miles from their home pasture.

Another small band released southeast of Miles City in the Blue Mountains swam the Yellowstone River and wandered almost 75 miles to the Circle area. Then they turned back, recrossed the Yellowstone and returned to the transplant site. A similar pattern occurred in a herd planted in the mountains near Anaconda. Soon after their release, sheep showed up on the airport, in yards at the west end of Anaconda, and some even wandered as far as the town of Warm Springs — about 10 miles to the east. Eventually the sheep returned on their own to the transplant site, where they became established.

Since bighorn permits are issued on the basis of specific districts, it isn't hard to locate the animals. Indeed, some of the herds spend a good part of the year adjacent to public roadways and are in easy viewing distance much of the year. But generally they're at the more remote parts of their range in the fall when hunting season opens — usually Sept. 15, but there are a few districts that open on other dates.

Hunting regulations are strict regarding sheep, particularly in the unlimited areas. In some districts hunters are required to present, within 10 days of the kill, the complete head and cape of their trophy to any Fish, Wildlife and Parks office or any game warden for tagging and issuance of a possession and transportation permit.

Another point to note concerning the unlimited districts, of which hunters should be aware, is that any ram taken is counted against a predetermined quota for the district and as soon as that quota is reached, the season in that district will be closed on 48 hours' notice. This can be within a few days of the season opening, so hunters are advised to inquire about the current status of the harvest at any time during the hunting season at the appropriate office of the Montana Department of Fish, Wildlife and Parks.

In the unlimited districts, the hunter has only 48 hours after the kill in which to **personally** present the complete head and cape to officials nearest the kill site, again for purposes of tagging and issuance of a possession and transportation permit.

Two other regulations for which hunters are strictly held accountable are that, 1. Any hunter with a license for a "legal ram" must not alter the head and horns as to make determination of legality uncertain, and 2. Hunters must, on demand, return to the kill site for inspection and show the complete head. This latter requirement is, of course, intended to prevent the taking of sheep in districts other than those in which the permit is held.

Again, seasons vary from year to year and in some districts adult ewes may be taken, in others only rams, and in others either sex. Hunters have to check the maps from year to year to determine what is allowed in the districts they want to seek permits for.

Chapter 9

Bowhunting in Montana

No aspect of hunting in Montana has grown in popularity as quickly as bowhunting. A revival of the ancient art of hunting big game with the bow and arrow that began in earnest in the 1950s has literally boomed in recent years so that bowhunting is one of the most avidly pursued dimensions of hunting in Montana.

Numbers give an idea of what has happened to bowhunting since 535 archery licenses were sold in Montana in 1953, the first year any special archery licenses were offered. Three years later, in 1956, the first statewide archery season for deer was conducted. That year 1,453 archery permits were purchased in Montana. The figure had skyrocketed to more than 10,000 in 1984. That's a phenomenal increase in a time period when the total number of hunting licenses sold only increased by half that much.

Part of bowhunting's popularity rests with the increased time out of doors it gives the sportsman. Many hunters now take advantage of that additional time in the field. Another is that technology has put the techniques of bowhunting within the grasp of many people, particularly compound bows that don't require physical strength to operate. The major reason for bowhunting's popularity is, however, twofold: It is both challenging and exciting. It puts the hunter to a greater test of skill than does rifle hunting.

Two other reasons, and they're major ones, that bowhunting has gained popularity in Montana has been the presence since 1973 of the Montana Bowhunters Association as a focal point of bowhunting interests and

Photo courtesy Greg Munther

Highly skilled and dedicated to technical detail, Greg Munther is one of Montana's most consistently successful bowhunters. Here he's shown with a fine bull elk he took in the typical sort of lodgepole cover they like once hunters get in the field.

the presence of one incredible leader at the helm of that outfit in the late 1970s and early 1980s — Lee Poole of Ennis. I doubt that any individual ever contributed more in terms of energy and expertise to the legitimizing of a hunting sport than Poole did for bowhunting in Montana during his tenure as president of the MBA.

Poole was joined, however, by hundreds of dedicated bowhunters statewide and they've been extremely aggressive in defending their sport and pursuing expansion of the bowhunting seasons. "We are a political type organization," Gene Wensel, an MBA board member, said. "Our purpose is to get good laws and to fight for bowhunter's rights."

At the same time, however, the organization has held clinics around the state and countless meetings to educate new bowhunters about ethics and political involvement as well as the art of bowhunting. "The future of bowhunting concerns us all," Poole said, "It's growing by leaps and bounds, but for it to survive we have to police our own ranks, educate bowhunters, particularly the new ones, and inform the public about what bowhunting is and how we go about it." In recent years, bowhunting in Montana has gone from its status in the 1960s as a tolerated "extra" for a few diehards to a sport enjoyed by many thousands. It also has developed one of the best organized, most effective lobbying voices in the state for sound wildlife management and hunting regulations.

To some the growth of interest in bowhunting is a puzzle. It has achiev-

Henry Schwenke of Sidney displays the "Bowhunter of the Year" plaque awarded him in 1979 by the Montana Bowhunter's Association. Schwenke is one of the pioneer bowhunters in Montana and told an interviewer he'll hunt "as long as I can pull a bow."

ed its popularity in spite of the fact that successful bowhunting is hard work requiring much more dedication, patience, persistence and field skill than rifle hunting.

That success isn't a mystery to two of the state's longtime bowhunters and active advocates of the sport, however — both of whom have been recognized by the Montana Bowhunters Association with its "Bowhunter of the Year Award." They are Jack Whitney of Bigfork and Henry Schwenke of Sidney.

Jack Whitney was the first recipient of that award and although he hasn't hunted in recent years, he has over a half a century of experience bowhunting in Montana. His name is written in the record books on almost every species taken with the bow; he's listed under bear, mountain lion, typical whitetail and mountain goat. At one time six of the nine mountain goats he's taken with bow and arrow were listed in the Pope and Young record book for Montana. He thinks the challenge of taking trophy game with a bow is the major attractant of the sport.

Schwenke, who does not hunt for trophies but rather for meat, says he thinks the closeness to nature realized during the bowhunter's time spent on stands or stalking animals is the major factor in bowhunting's popularity. Schwenke began hunting in 1956 and does most of his hunting in the open prairie and breaks country of eastern Montana. He related that one of his biggest thrills as a bowhunter was watching his son Dwight take a 5x6 bull elk in 1983 in the Missouri Breaks.

Bowhunter Stoney Burk is all smiles as he poses with the six-point bull elk he took after several gruelling days of hunting in the heavily-timbered basins of northwestern Montana.

The fact that bowhunters become intimately involved with the area they hunt and the species they go after pervades the activity. Serious bowhunters spend countless hours afield in the off-season studying the animals they hunt and developing a detailed understanding of their habits and the places they live. To some, that is fully as enjoyable as the actual hunt.

"My guess is that the vast, vast majority of my time was spent observing rather than actually hunting," Whitney said. "I just enjoyed being out there." An article written for the MBA newsletter about Bob Savage of Bozeman, who is considered among serious bowhunters as one of the finest bowhunters in the world, gives clear insight regarding this phenomenon:

"Unlike the bulk of bowhunters, Bob Savage is a full-time hunter and a part-time archer. At face value this may confuse many but it will make sense once we examine it further. How do we justify calling ourselves hunters by merely practicing shooting at a bale of straw for a month? Bob takes every spare moment to be afield 'hunting' without bow, learning the habits of game and to practice stalking to within easy bow range."

Part of that sensitivity is passed from generation to generation of bowhunters, however, as mentioned by Henry.Schwenke in regard to his thrill at being with his son on the taking of a bull elk. The link from one generation to another was also highlighted in an article for the MBA publication by Bob Beck of Ennis.

"Bob (Savage) credits his development as a bow builder and hunter to Jack Whitney. When Bob was 9 or 10, Jack noted his interest in bow-building and helped Bob refine his techniques. Jack helped him set goals in developing bows and got him interested in the hunting of big game."

I can attest to that link, too. It was Jack Whitney who got me interested in bowhunting years ago when I lived in the Flathead Valley. Many is the hour I've enjoyed listening to Jack tell of stalks and stands he's made on elk or, his specialty, mountain goats. Always it was the essence of his relationship to the wildlife and the absolute awe he held for them that in turn intrigued me. I owe much of my early interest in observing wildlife for the joy of it to Whitney, who has remained a close friend over the years.

Lee Poole suggested that other factors join that of emotional satisfaction. "We have the finest bowhunting opportunities in the country," he said during an interview at the MBA convention in Butte in 1984, which incidentally attracted more than 2,000 bowhunters. "Our seasons are five to five and a half weeks long."

The other is the variety of game that can be hunted with the bow, a point that internationally-known bowhunting expert Gene Wensel of Hamilton emphasized. "The biggest thing is the variety of game," Wensel said. "It is exceptional that way." So is the record potential, however. In 1981 David Snyder took a Pope and Young world record bull elk in the Little Belt Mountains of Montana. The 6x6 bull scored 391 6/8 points.

Photo courtesy Greg Munther

This bowhunter is about to take a black bear that has come to the edge of an opening and which was unaware that the hunter had been waiting for it to make a move from the heavy timber at left.

On the whole, however, Montana is noted more for its general overall hunting quality than for its contribution to world bowhunting records. Wensel suggested that individuals wanting bigger mule deer trophies might be better off going to Colorado, while those simply wanting a nice mule deer probably could do better in Utah. Antelope hunters, conversely, would find better trophy chances in Wyoming.

For sheer variety, however, he'd have to recommend Montana. Bowhunters can pursue 11 species of big game — elk, mule deer, whitetail deer, antelope, black bear, grizzly bear, mountain lion, bighorn sheep, mountain goat, moose and bison. And while most Montana hunters are more meat conscious and thereby more concerned with taking an animal rather than pursuing a trophy-book head, the chances of trophies are always there.

Marion James, publisher of *Bowhunter Magazine,* said Montana's reputation among bowhunters nationally is exaggerated — mainly because of the kind of press it has received in publications that emphasize the taking of animals and not the amount of effort that has to go into getting them. His observations are borne out by success statistics, too, which indicate that only 10 to 12 percent of those who hunt deer with the bow get animals and only 5 to 6 percent of the elk hunters score.

"I think the perspective most bowhunters nationally have of Montana is distorted," James said. "Most people think there's an animal behind every

One of the premiere bowhunters in the country, Ron Granneman of Great Falls, Montana, has taken a trophy bull elk almost every season and he makes a special effort to put himself into good, isolated hunting country.

tree and those of us who have hunted out here know that isn't true. Bowhunting is a challenging, difficult sport and when people think of coming out to Montana, it's to find animals everywhere. When they don't, they're disappointed."

James said the general view in the bowhunting fraternity nationally ranks Montana second behind Colorado among western states. "For my own opinion, hunting in Montana may be superior to that found in Colorado," James said, "but Colorado gets better press."

The points James raised are valid, however. It is human nature — and undeniably a hunter's nature — to emphasize the good and forget the bad and we need look no further than our photographs to prove it. We focus on the notion of our trophies rather than the entire hunting experience and in this aspect of the bowhunter's life, he or she is no different from rifle hunters.

The increase in bowhunting everywhere, including Montana, is directly related to the difficulty it affords. Buck Damone of Lewistown, who was elected president of the MBA in 1984 to replace Poole, emphasized a conviction that it is precisely because people want greater challenges that they are willing to pursue big game with bow and arrow. Most of them measure the "success" of their undertaking with a profound acceptance of the odds against them.

Still, most bowhunters keep careful records of their hunts and the trophies they take and many, if not most, of the leaders in the bowhunting

The edges of small meadows like this are excellent places to establish a blind and wait for elk. Tracks in the wallows at this site indicated used of the area not only by elk but by deer and bear.

fraternity have their names listed in the trophy books. For example, Buck Damone's name is listed under several species. So are the names of Bob Savage and Lee Poole, Scott Koelzer of Bozeman, Paul Schafer of Whitefish, Ron Granneman of Great Falls, Greg Munther of Missoula, Paul Bruner of Ovando, and the Wensel brothers — Barry of Whitefish and Gene of Hamilton. The list could go on and on.

Some species listings are dominated by a few individuals — David Snyder and Ron Granneman in elk, James Dean in mule deer, Gene Wensel in whitetail deer, and Jack Whitney in mountain goat.

Of the species hunted in Montana, the consensus among expert bowhunters is that the trophy whitetail buck is the most difficult to take. "Antelope are probably the second hardest to get in the trophy class and elk are probably the easiest, but that's only comparative," Whitney said. "They're all hard to get, whoever is doing the hunting."

Gene Wensel, who has taken several whitetail bucks listed in the trophy book, is joined by many bowhunting addicts who believe that the next world record whitetail buck will come from Montana. Whitetails are a passion to Wensel. He is recognized as one of the country's top experts on the subject and has authored a book, *Hunting Rutting Whitetails*, that has become a classic in its field.

The techniques of bowhunting vary from person to person and the type of bow used, but the fundamentals are the same: practice, practice and practice again. Learn the species hunted and its habits. Learn to become stealthy and woods-wise. Respect and follow the rules of fair chase and game laws. Know how an arrow works and never shoot unless you can make a good shot. Practice bowhunting safety (bowhunting is hazardous — you're dealing with razor-sharp arrowheads).

The advent of thousands of new bowhunters to the field has some of the sport's leaders concerned — mainly because too many new people have been coming into the sport too fast to give all of them the sort of training they need. The result has been that many new bowhunters go afield without first acquiring either the skill or sense of bowhunting ethics they need. In some cases the sport has been given a bad name by the activities of these neophytes — particularly those who tend to shoot when they shouldn't and those who have neither the skill nor tendency to properly track wounded game.

Bowhunting clinics by the MBA and assistance from the Montana Department of Fish, Wildlife and Parks have helped improve this situation. So have communication efforts by other sportsman's organizations and such national groups as the National Bowhunter Education Foundation.

A bow and arrow hunter in Montana is required to purchase a "Bow and Arrow" license or "stamp" in addition to the license for each species hunted. In 1984 the cost of these were $6 for both resident and nonresident. These licenses apply to the taking of big game animals during the regular archery season and a number of special seasons established in specific districts from year to year.

Archery hunters can hunt throughout the bow and arrow season and the general season, with one major difference. During the archery season the bowhunter can go afield in any sort of clothing, but during the general season the archer is required to wear 400 square inches of blaze orange material above the waist just as the rifle hunter is.

Hunter success, when measured by the percentage of animals taken against the number of hunters who went afield, has always been low among bowhunters — a clear indication that much more than killing game is involved with the measurement of success when afield with the bow. Even so, harvest statistics compiled by the Montana Department of Fish, Wildlife and Parks for the 1983 season, the latest information available, give a good picture of archery hunting across the state:

Bowhunting Hunter Success Figures

Region	Mule Deer	Whitetail Deer	Elk	Antelope
1	7%	10%	6%	0%
2	15%	11%	4%	0%
3	14%	11%	7%	16%
4	14%	6%	6%	26%
5	18%	12%	5%	16%
6	18%	9%	0%	14%
7	23%	13%	6%	23%

Gene Wensel of Hamilton, Montana, with one of the many trophy whitetail bucks he has taken with the bow. Wensel is one of the nation's most respected bowhunters and through his writings and lectures has helped elevate trophy whitetail buck hunting to a high art.

Chapter 10

Applying for and Getting a Permit

As recent as 1980, your odds weren't too bad in terms of getting a special permit for either-sex elk, antelope or either-sex deer in Montana hunting districts where such permits were available. The law of averages gave you a good chance of getting an antelope permit or extra deer at least every other year and a special elk permit about every third year. Then the permit situation got wild, and difficult, as thousands upon thousands **more** hunters began applying for permits.

Consider, for example, the situation regarding either-sex elk permits. In 1980 only 41,668 individuals applied for 11,662 available permits. In 1981, 52,689 applied. By 1983 the figure was up to 75,486, and in 1984 the figure was 228,134 — up 33 percent in one year.

Still, it's not as difficult to get one of the common-game permits as it always has been to draw one of the more rare and highly sought after "trophy" permits — those bighorn sheep, mountain goat and moose. Those have always been hard to get, generally well under 10 percent.

Getting a permit isn't a cinch for any species, however, and more than one complaint has come into the Special License Bureau of the Montana Fish, Wildlife and Parks from individuals who have never drawn one. Some people just can't seem to get the luck of the draw — particularly in regard to the trophy species. I know. I'm one of them. I've never been able to get a moose or bighorn sheep permit, though I've sure tried often enough. On the other hand, I have no complaints in regard to deer and special elk permits. My success there is about even with the odds everyone has enjoyed, or suffered, depending on your perspective.

Jim Herman, chief of the License Bureau for the Montana Department of Fish, Wildlife and Parks, keeps careful records of such things and advises that one's chances relate directly to the mathematical odds involved. Thus, the probability of your name being drawn will depend entirely upon how much competition you face for both the species and district in which you apply.

For example, you might want to apply only in a specific district where lots of other people also apply, yet with only a few permits to be won, the odds are really against you. On the opposite side of the ledger, often the department doesn't fill the number of Deer B tags or antelope tags in some eastern Montana districts that are remote from the state's population centers. Apply there and you'll likely get a permit, but also plan on a long drive if you decide to use it.

On a statewide basis, the following chart will give you an idea of what your statistical chances are from species to species. The data cover the last five years:

PERCENT SUCCESSFUL - PERMIT DRAWINGS

Species	1980	1981	1982	1983	1984
Antelope	50%	51%	60%	61%	69%
Deer A	0	60	94	65	55
Deer B	72	72	80	78	92
Elk Permit	28	24	21	22	24
Deer Permit	41	54	48	21	4
Moose	3	3	3	3	4
Sheep	11	12	13	10	14
Goat	6	6	6	6	7
Average Total	32%	34%	37%	39%	46%

Applying for a permit is almost as easy as it sounds, and almost as difficult. First, you have to get application forms — which are different for resident and nonresident hunters — from the department or, in the case of residents, from a license agent. Then you have to fill them in and submit them by a cutoff date, which historically has been June 15 but which was moved up to June 1 in 1985. Even that might change, however, so again you're advised to check the regulations from year to year.

That done, all you have to do is sit back and wait for the computerized drawing to take place in August, right? Wrong. There's more to it than waiting to see if you get a mailing from the Department of Fish, Wildlife and Parks — which means you get a permit — or from the Department of Revenue, which means you get a refund because you failed to draw a permit. Before any of that can take place, you've got to make sure your application is properly filled out or you won't even get your name in the drawings.

Herman advises that each year more than 3,000 permit applications

Massive curls of horns and the thick-bodied heft of a mature Montana bighorn sheep shows why this animal is among the state's most sought-after permit animals. Several sheep hunting districts in the state are characterized by such difficult hunting terrain that unlimited permits are available in them.

don't even get into the selection process because the individuals submitting them missed the mailing deadline or didn't provide the right information on the application form. And once your name is tossed out, for any reason, you're out for that year. Period.

"We find it frustrating to deal with errors because we hate to see anybody get eliminated from the drawings for missing even mandatory information," Herman said, "and we do try to fill in minimum information if it's readily available. But if it involves a judgment, like listing a district, we don't do it because we can't anticipate what a hunter wants."

Herman provided statistics for the "error count" in 1983, the last year for which detailed statistics are available. Some 3,043 individuals failed to get their names into the drawing for one reason or another, and that was a decline from the year before when 3,109 were tossed out for most of the same reasons.

Why are so many people eliminated from the drawings? The 1983 statistics are revealing. There were 218,256 total applications, so the 3,043 represented a fairly small percentage of people who fouled up — 1.3 percent. Of these, 1,013 failed to enclose sufficient money to cover the application fees for the permits they hoped to get. Another 683 individuals failed to sign their applications, even though it's clearly printed on the application form that "Incomplete or incorrect applications will not be entered into the drawing."

Another 261 individuals failed to enclose any money at all, one failed

Box upon box upon box of permit applications literally flood the Department of Fish, Wildlife and Parks every year. Here's just part of the stack in a recent year and more come in every year. In 1984, 229,134 applications for permits were received.

to give an address and 74 submitted their names but didn't fill in the application form itself. They didn't apply for anything. Some 88 rejections involved the submission of a nonresident license with a personal check; a money order, cash or cashier's check is required.

A common failing was missing the application deadline — 823 did that. Herman related that an interesting fact of the permit application process is that a vast majority of people wait until three or four days before the deadline to send in their application forms.

Most mysterious of all were some 39 application envelopes which made it in on time but had nothing inside. Presumably, the would-be applicants had failed to enclose their applications.

Herman particularly cautioned younger nonresident applicants to be sure to list their Hunter Safety Number on the application. That number is required for all hunters under 18, but it is possible for the department to check only its records for resident applicants who fail to list the number. "If it was a nonresident application, it could not be processed as there is no listing available," Herman said. "Nonresidents, if under 18, **must** submit a photocopy (of their Hunter Safety Certificate) with their application at the time it is submitted.

Of particular importance on the applications are five "mandatory" steps that must be filled in or the application will not even be processed. They include the applicant's name and address, date of birth, conservation license number, phone number, and hunter safety number if under 18. In addition, the application must be signed. Here failure to sign the form or list the conservation number and birth date are the most common errors.

The permit system has contributed mightily to the coffers of the wildlife agency. In 1984, $1,780,084.00 for permits and $456,268.00 for drawing fees were taken in, compared to $1,019,875 for permits and $436,512 for the drawing fee in 1983. This is up from totals of $961,835 in 1982 and only $360,445 in 1980. Special permits have become big business.

Your chances of getting a permit can be enhanced, as implied earlier, by selecting districts where fewer people apply for a greater number of permits. An excellent source of information is a booklet issued annually by the Special Licensing Division titled *Drawing Statistics and Harvest Statistics*. It's available for $2.00 from the Special Licensing Division, Montana Department of Fish, Wildlife and Parks, 1420 East Sixth, Helena, MT 59620 and provides helpful information on which to base applications from district to district.

On the whole, here's what the odds charts show as your chances for drawing a permit for the various species:

Antelope

Year	1980	1981	1982	1983	1984
Applications	35,748	38,233	43,588	52,749	56,282
Permits	18,150	21,240	26,212	32,041	39,080
Percentage	50%	55%	60%	61%	65%

Deer A

Year	1980	1981	1982	1983	1984
Applications	-0-	662	1,186	4,007	8,502
Permits	-0-	394	1,114	2,592	4,733
Percentage	-0-	60%	94%	65%	55%

Deer B

Year	1980	1981	1982	1983	1984
Applications	7,197	13,080	21,007	36,542	44,389
Permits	5,190	9,472	16,895	28,634	40,757
Percentage	72%	72%	80%	78%	92%

Elk

Year	1980	1981	1982	1983	1984
Applications	41,668	52,689	64,775	75,486	81,098
Permits	11,662	12,455	13,550	16,285	19,260
Percentage	28%	24%	21%	22%	24%

Deer Permit

Year	1980	1981	1982	1983	1984
Applications	6,857	8,458	7,679	13,395	9,923
Permits	2,84?	4,571	3,659	2,850	400
Percentage	41%	54%	48%	21%	4%

Moose

Year	1980	1981	1982	1983	1984
Applications	19,623	18,479	18,233	21,051	16,109
Permits	537	532	577	588	645
Percentage	3%	3%	3%	3%	4%

Bighorn Sheep

Year	1980	1981	1982	1983	1984
Applications	7,360	6,846	6,741	8,170	7,147
Permits	823	784	902	1,106	744
Percentage	11%	12%	13%	14%	10%

Mountain Goat

Year	1980	1981	1982	1983	1984
Applications	6,730	6,267	5,918	6,856	4,685
Permits	374	364	338	330	351
Percentage	6%	6%	6	6%	7%

Totals — All Species

Year	1980	1981	1982	1983	1984
Applications	125,183	144,704	169,117	169,117	228,134
Permits	39,579	49,812	63,247	84,419	105,970
Percentage	32%	34%	37%	39%	46%

Herman also suggests that applicants pay close attention to the hunter harvest statistics in the districts for which permits are given. This gives the hunter a sense of what sort of success he or she might expect **if** a permit is drawn. To help in this determination, Herman's division has drawn up these helpful statistics from the 1983 season, the latest available:

Moose

0-20% Hunter Success — Hunting district 314-02.

21-40% Hunter Success — Hunting districts 311-02, 350, 512, 515.

41-60% Hunter Success — Hunting districts 210, 308-02, 312, 313-01, 313-02, 316-02, 317, 513, 514, 516.

61-80% Hunter Success — Hunting districts 120, 150, 211, 212, 270, 292, 3021, 306-02, 310,02, 311,01, 314-01, 315-01, 315-02, 318-01, 360.

81-100% Hunter Success — Hunting districts 100, 101, 102, 103, 110, 121, 140, 214, 215, 230, 240, 250, 261, 301, 306-01, 308-01, 309-01, 310-01, 316-01, 318-02, 319-01, 319-02, 321-01, 321-02, 322-01, 322-02, 323-01, 323-02, 324, 330, 331, 333, 334, 340, 361-01, 361-02, 380.

Bighorn Sheep

0-20% Hunter Success — Hunting districts 250, 300-01, 301,m 302, 303, 500, 501, 502.

Photo by Neal Mischler

The Shiras moose found in Montana may not be as massive as other species of this awesome big game animal, but it still is a tremendous trophy hunted in the Big Sky Country only on drawn permit.

21-40% Hunter Success — Hunting district 270-01.

41-60% Hunter Success — Hunting districts 123-01, 123-02.

61-80% Hunter Success — Hunting districts 100-02, 213-01, 213-02, 455.

81-100% Hunter Success — 100-01, 121-01, 121-02, 122-02, 216-01, 216-02, 270-02, 340-01, 340-02, 421,01, 421-02, 422-01, 422-01, 423-01, 423-02, 424-01, 424-02, 500-01, 620, 760.

In addition, no data was available for districts 122-01, 203 and 441-01.

Mountain Goat

0-20% Hunter Success — Hunting districts 140, 151, 321, 451.

21-40% Hunter Success — Hunting districts 131, 132, 142, 222.

41-60% Hunter Success — Hunting districts 130, 141, 220, 250, 261, 280, 320.

61-80% Hunter Success — Hunting districts 100, 223, 240, 312, 322, 323, 447, 514, 517, 518.

81-100% Hunter Success — Hunting districts 101, 133, 150, 213, 270, 325, 331, 380, 393, 414, 415, 431, 446, 516, 519.

Antelope

0-20% Hunter Success — Hunting districts 321-02, 380-01, 720.

21-40% Hunter Success — No districts listed in this category.

41-60% Hunter Success — Hunting districts 318, 440, 610.

61-80% Hunter Success — Hunting districts 300, 311, 319, 329, 330, 341, 350, 400, 401, 410, 420-01, 430, 444, 450, 470, 500-01, 510-01, 511, 512, 513-01, 514, 530, 572, 620, 630, 640, 650, 721, 732, 733, 740, 733, 740, 750, 760, 761, 782.

81-100% Hunter Success — Hunting districts 301, 310, 320, 321-01, 338, 339, 340, 360, 370, 380-02, 3890-03, 380-04, 380-05, 390, 420-02, 455, 460, 471, 473, 490, 491, 501-01, 540, 550, 560, 570, 571, 590-01, 600, 611, 612, 670, 680, 690, 711, 712, 713, 714, 715, 722, 741, 743, 744, 745.

101% or More Hunter Success — Hunting districts 480, 481-01, 481-02, 481-03, 500-02, 501-02, 510-02, 513-02, 590-02, 700, 710, 730, 731, 742, 781, 783, 790, 791. In these districts, hunter success can exceed 100 percent because a hunter can kill one antelope on the first tag and another with a second tag, providing the possibility of two antelope per hunter.

Elk

The following pertains to hunter success for all elk hunters during the fall 1983 hunting season, the latest for which statistics are available:

0-5% Hunter Success — Hunting districts 100, 101, 102, 120, 122, 130, 204, 240, 281, 284, 415, 420, 427, 441, 448, 510, 560.

6-10% Hunter Success — Hunting districts 103, 110, 200, 201, 203, 210, 212, 214, 261, 270, 283, 291, 292, 293, 302, 319, 331, 414, 418, 429, 432, 435, 442, 443, 454, 520, 521, 540, 562, 572.

11-15% Hunter Success — Hunting districts 121, 140, 141, 151, 213, 250, 301, 310, 313, 315, 316, 318, 320, 322, 326, 340, 350, 361, 370, 392, 416, 422, 424, 425, 428, 449, 452, 455, 513, 514, 561, 581.

Deer

This data pertains to hunter success for all hunters for the fall 1983 hunting season, the latest for which data was available.

0-10% Hunter Success — No districts listed in this category.

11-20% Hunter Success — Hunting districts 213, 214, 261, 321, 332.

21-30% Hunter Success — Hunting districts 110, 120, 140, 141, 200, 203, 204, 211, 215, 216, 240, 250, 270, 280, 284, 290, 291, 293, 310, 316, 318, 319, 327, 350, 361, 362, 429, 435, 448, 455.

31-40% Hunter Success — Hunting districts 102, 122, 130, 150, 151, 201, 202, 212, 260, 281, 283, 292, 300, 301, 312, 323, 324, 328, 329, 340, 341, 370, 380, 390, 392, 415, 423, 425, 432, 441, 443,

513, 550.

41-50% Hunter Success — Hunting districts 100, 101, 103, 121, 210, 302, 322, 325, 331, 333, 360, 391, 393, 403, 416, 420, 422, 424, 428, 442, 449.

51-60% Hunter Success — Hunting districts 282, 311, 313, 314, 317, 320, 326, 406, 413, 418, 421, 444, 445, 446a, 452, 454, 472, 510, 521, 522, 540, 621, 623, 632.

61-70% Hunter Success — Hunting districts 315, 400, 401, 404, 405, 410, 414, 417, 427, 447, 450, 500, 501, 502, 511, 514, 520, 530, 560, 562, 580, 591, 612, 631, 640, 641, 710, 713, 714, 733, 743, 750, 761.

71-80% Hunter Success — Hunting districts 402, 411, 412, 419, 426, 471, 561, 570, 571, 572, 573, 574, 581, 582, 590, 592, 590, 592, 600, 610, 611, 620, 622, 630, 650, 670, 680, 690, 691, 711, 712, 715, 720, 721, 722, 730, 731, 732, 740, 741, 742, 760, 770, 771, 772, 780, 782, 792.

100% or More Hunter Success — Hunting districts 700, 744, 745, 773, 781, 790, 791. Hunter success could exceed 100% in these districts because a hunter could get a two-deer license in them.

Black Bear Spring Season

0-10% Hunter Success — Hunting districts 101, 103, 141, 151, 200, 203, 210, 213, 216, 240, 250, 260, 270, 281, 282, 284, 292, 293, 300, 301, 302, 310, 312, 316, 320, 324, 325, 326, 327, 328, 329, 341, 361, 370, 380, 390, 391, 393, 400, 401, 402, 403, 404, 405, 406, 410, 412, 413, 414, 415, 417, 418, 419, 420, 421, 422, 423, 424, 425, 426, 427, 428, 429, 432, 435, 442, 444, 445, 447, 448, 449, 450, 452, 454, 455, 471, 472, 500, 501, 502, 510, 511, 513, 514, 530, 540, 560, 561, 562, 570, 571, 573, 574, 580, 581, 590, 592.

11-20% Hunter Success — Hunting districts 100, 102, 110, 130, 201, 204, 212, 291, 311, 314, 315, 319, 333, 360, 362, 411, 521, 550, 582.

21-30% Hunter Success — Hunting districts 121, 122, 150, 211, 214, 215, 283, 313, 318, 321, 322, 331, 340, 416, 443, 522, 572.

31-40% Hunter Success — Hunting districts 202, 317, 392, 446, 520.

41% and More Hunter Success — Hunting districts 140, 261, 280, 290, 323, 332, 350.

Black Bear Fall Season

0-10% Hunter Success — Hunting districts 110, 122, 130, 140, 141, 150, 151, 200, 203, 204, 210, 212, 213, 214, 215, 216, 240, 250, 260, 261, 270, 280, 290, 291, 293, 300, 301, 293, 300, 301, 302,

310, 311, 312, 313, 314, 315, 316, 317, 318, 319, 320, 321, 322, 323, 324, 325, 326, 327, 328, 331, 333, 340, 341, 350, 360, 361, 362, 370, 380, 390, 391, 392, 400, 401, 402, 403, 404, 405, 406, 410, 412, 413, 415, 416, 417, 418, 419, 420, 421, 422, 423, 424, 426, 427, 428, 429, 432, 435, 441, 442, 443, 444, 446, 447, 448, 449, 450, 452, 454, 455, 471, 472, 500, 501, 510, 511, 513, 514, 520, 521, 522, 530, 540, 550, 560, 561, 562, 570, 571, 572, 573, 574, 580, 581, 582, 590, 591, 592.

11-20% Hunter Success — Hunting districts 100, 101, 102, 103, 120, 121, 201, 202, 211, 283, 292, 329, 332, 414.

21-30% Hunter Success — Hunting districts 282, 284, 411, 425, 445, 502.

31-40% Hunter Success — Hunting district 393.

41% or More Hunter Success — No districts listed in this category.

Turkey

Region One
Hunting Districts 121 and 122, Spring season by special permit only, no fall season.

Region Four
Chouteau County, spring season by special permit only, no fall season.

Region Five
Big Horn County, 33.33% in spring season, 47.62% in fall season.

Golden Valley County, no spring season, 0% in fall season. Musselshell County, no spring season, 47.12% in fall season.

Yellowstone County, no spring season, 0% in fall season.

Region Six
McCone County, 0% in spring season, no fall season.

Region Seven
Carter County, 34.78% in spring season, 48.78% in fall season.

Custer County, no spring season, 60.29% in fall season.

Dawson County, no spring season, 57.14% in fall season.

Fallon County, no spring season, 45.10% in fall season.

Garfield County, 31.58% in spring season, 40.30% in fall season.

Powder River County, 33.33% in spring season, 55.89% in fall season.

Prairie County, no spring season, 63.41% in fall season.

Rosebud County, 24% in spring season, 27.27% in fall season.

Treasure County, no spring season, 0% in fall season.

Wibaux County, no spring season, 0% in fall season.

Chapter 11

Landowner-Sportsman Relations

Of all the issues affecting sportsmen, that of landowner-sportsman relations is the most frustrating to deal with. It seems that no matter how much effort is put into making things work between the two parties, something always comes up to cause a division.

Perhaps it will always be that way. It is the sort of problem that really is a complex of interrelated brush fires rather than one major problem, so it is a conundrum — an issue that can't really be solved. No sooner is one aspect of the dilemma dealt with when the same thing crops up somewhere else. Thus, the sum of all the parts has made the question of access **the** major problem of Montana sportsmen.

Still, it is encouraging that people and organizations on both sides of the landowner-sportsman question are working toward at least making things better. If we can't expect the issue to go away, and we can't, at least those involved can cooperate to deal with aspects of the problem and not let it destroy or diminish outdoor recreation in Montana.

Ron Marcoux, associate director of the Montana Department of Fish, Wildife and Parks, emphasized that with 65 percent of Montana hunting lands on private property, the question takes on two dimensions — the landowners' relations with hunters and their attitude about wildlife. "One of our biggest problems is to recognize that hunting opportunities aren't infinite," Marcoux said. "The direction we go today in dealing with these problems will determine what kind of hunting we will have in the future."

Among the dozens of landowners, hunters and resource managers I talked to statewide regarding this issue, the positive approach to solving it

The use of a boat for access to country adjacent to the Missouri and other big rivers in Montana has proven for some to be an excellent hunting technique. This party of successful mule deer hunters were on an outfitted trip with Craig Madsen's Great Adventures West of Great Falls. Be sure to check regulations for boat use and access on lands adjacent to the streams you float hunt.

was perhaps best summed up by Harley Yeager of Great Falls, who, as an information and education officer for the Montana Department of Fish, Wildife and Parks Department, has long been recognized for his efforts to alleviate landowner-sportsman conflicts. "We're really hot on this issue out here (northcentral Montana) because most of the land we deal with is private land," Yeager said. "We go out of our way to work with the landowner, because out here they realize and we realize that if we can control the hunter's vehicle, we can control the problem."

The solution in Yeager's area has been the development of a form used by landowners to grant written permission to hunt on their land. It has three copies, one of which goes to the sportsman, one to the landowner and the third to the local game warden. If a problem comes up and the sportsman doesn't have that permit, he doesn't belong on that property.

"It doesn't solve everything, but it does get at the heart of the matter, which is the legal requirement that hunters get a landowner's permission before they hunt on his property," Yeager said. "It has proven to be a way of meeting the needs of the landowners to know who's on their property and the hunters in terms of getting them access to many places they otherwise couldn't hunt."

For the sportsman, the issue most often is access to hunt and fish not.

only on private land where game is found but also to go through that land to gain access to public land beyond. For the landowners, it is the recognition of ownership rights and protection of their property both in terms of what is done on it and to it. The fact is that in all too many cases, the landowners' complaints are that their property has been abused and that their rights to control their own resources has been violated.

Fortunately, most landowners and most sportsmen realize that the source of the majority of their problems involves the actions of only a few slob hunters. The question facing both, then, is how to best deal with those few hunters who cause the problems — a situation made more difficult because those few slob hunters most often have long fled the scene when their offenses are discovered by the landowner.

Some offenses can be costly to the landowner. Livestock killed, gates left open, fences torn down, trash left to litter the landowner's property, shooting in the vicinity of livestock or buildings, vehicles driven off established roadways, people hunting in areas they shouldn't, and so on, ad infinitum. These problems are common throughout the state.

One other problem, however, stems from the effort of sportsmen to practice the so-called "Three C's" of landowner-sportsman relationships: courtesy, consideration and common sense. That is the question of "bother". I know it is a bother for a landowner to have to deal with my phone call when I phone to ask permission to hunt on his land or when I stop by his house. I know others are doing the same, intruding on his early morning or evening because that's generally the only time we can get to him. But we also know that many landowners want game populations reduced on their property, so we call to get permission to hunt.

I asked a rancher in the area north of Jordan about the problem of bother. "Go ahead and call," he said. "We generally feel your intentions are good if you guys call us beforehand." Then he asked me not to put his name in this book. "I've got enough guys calling me now," he said. So bother really was an issue to him and I concluded that we sportsmen need to use real consideration of the landowners' time when it comes to making that contact with him.

I couldn't help, however, remembering a letter a rancher sent to the Montana Fish, Wildlife and Parks Department in which this issue was addressed. I repeat a portion of it here because it puts the problem in perspective:

"Beginning by September, and increasingly through October and into November, we are besieged by phone calls and visits from prospective hunters hoping to find game and a place to hunt it. During the past four years, we have averaged approximately 1,000,that's one thousand, hunter days on our ranch. Understandably, most hunters call or stop by to ask where the deer are, where the closed areas are, where the other hunters are, etc., etc., etc., Consider that 1,000 hunters visiting only five minutes each = 5,000 minutes = 83 hours = for, example, two

The proliferation of mule deer throughout much of central and eastern Montana has necessitated the use of extra, B-tag, permits to harvest does in areas where the deer have outstripped the resource base. Here Bruce Burk of Missoula and Ted Burk of Stevensville are shown with a mule deer Bruce took as part of a reduction program on a ranch along the Judith River in northcentral Montana.

average work weeks. (Not even to mention the inevitable sustained damages and frustrations caused by (only) a few hunters; consider that if only four percent of 1,000 hunters are careless, that's 40 hunters or, on the average, an incident every day during the season.) P.S. In general, we like hunters."

This particular rancher encourages hunting on the land, but like most landowners he sets some conditions. Here's what he wants from hunters: "This year, we are going to ask you to do three things in exchange for the privilege of hunting on our ranch: 1. Try hard to take a deer or antelope off our range (any age or sex will do) consistent with the law; 2. Abide by our rules and signs; 3. Seriously consider purchasing an additional 70 pounds of beef from your grocer during the next year for each animal you take home this season." (Note — Those beef purchases help ranchers survive economically.)

James Flynn, director of the MDWF&P, says about the same thing at the start of every hunting season when he issues his annual plea to sportsmen to respect the rights of landowners. I've saved a number of those press releases from the past few years. They're generally entitled something like "Cooperate With Private Landowners" and they "urge Montana sportsmen to work for new levels of cooperation with private landowners during this fall's hunting seasons."

Flynn then offers several : suggestions for those who intend to hunt on private land. They are: 1. Ask the landowner's permission to hunt on or cross his property, preferably in advance; 2. Use established roads and do not drive through crops or pastures; 3. Leave gates as they are found; 4. Don't litter; 5. Be careful with firearms, particularly around livestock, buildings, and, most of all, people; 6. Report any violations you see to law enforcement officials, game wardens or the Department of Fish, Wildlife and Parks on the toll free line, 800-332-6117.

"The observance of these rules of courtesy and common sense will go a long way toward convincing landowners to extend hunting and fishing privileges to Montana sportsmen," Flynn said. "Hunting as we know it in Montana depends on access to private land, and every sportsman assumes the responsibility to respect the rights of property owners."

Over the years, the wildlife agency has worked closely with sportsman's groups, hunting and fishing clubs and organizations like the Montana Wildlife Federation, individual landowners and organizations like the Montana Stockgrowers Association to deal positively with the question of landowner-sportsman relations. Now its efforts have taken a new twist in the form of a structured program called the Cooperative Landowner-Sportsman's program, which is headed up by a full-time staff director in Helena.

"The problem of access is now beginning to be felt in Montana and we realize we need to provide a transition from resource managers who deal only with biology to those with sociological skills, too," Marcoux said. "We've got to learn to blend the social needs and issues with the biological world."

Basically, the program as intended works directly with issues of the sportsman relating to the landowner, but it has brought some new wrinkles to that relationship. Among them was an experimental program in southwestern Montana in 1984 in which hunters with permits in a special crop damage hunt were required to first check in with department personnel to be assigned a place to hunt. Thus, the landowner was freed from this administrative chore — and reports from both hunters and ranchers indicated that it worked well.

Other aspects of the new effort include plans to review laws covering trespass and liability to see if they provide adequate protection for the landowner, or if they need to be strengthened, to seek a larger legislative appropriation for game damage control, to investigate more effective techniques for repelling game animals from haystacks and crops, to examine the possibility of developing an insurance program to reimburse private landowners for livestock accidentally killed, and to emphasize hunter ethics training.

The new program grew out of earlier efforts of the Landowner Relations-Sportsman Access Advisory Council, which first convened in 1977 and led directly to the establishment of the statewide, toll-free number for reporting violations of game and trespass laws, a growing awareness of the need for self-policing among sportsmen and improved enforcement of fish and game laws, particularly those related to the public use of private land.

John Gilpatrick, a Hilger rancher who formerly served as a chairman of that council, lauded the role it served in terms of providing communication between the landowners and the state wildlife agency because there are no short-term solutions to the problem of sportsman access. "The problem has always been with us," Gilpatrick said. "The challenge is to maintain as much private land for public use as possible."

The new program has given hope to both sides of the issue because efforts are being made not only to talk about problems, but to do something to solve them. The "Ask First" program is an example. The Department of Fish, Wildlife and Parks and sportsman's groups distributed bumper sticks and erected signs in 1984 emphasizing the need for hunters to ask permission before they entered private land.

"Ask First to Hunt and Fish on Private Land" the stickers read. And it is a good start for getting at the root of landowner-sportsman problems. However, it is only a beginning. Kay Ellerhoff of the state wildlife agency put it well in a department statement advising hunters that they need to add "three more little words" to the message when relating to landowners. They are "Please" and "Thank You."

She didn't add that things would be a lot better for all sportsmen if each of us would use those three little words every time we related to a landowner.

Chapter 12

The Outfitted Hunt

Ever since Sir George Gore lavished his way in 1854 across part of the region that would become Montana, the outfitted hunt has been part of the state's hunting tradition. To be sure, no one any more sees the sort of extravagance that Sir George exhibited. Nonetheless, the outfitted hunt remains an entrenched part of the overall hunting picture.

Sir George, in fact, would have little in common with the average hunter today who seeks an outfitted trip. The European "gentleman hunter," as he labeled himself, didn't exactly like to rough it. He was accompanied by 41 men, four mule wagons, three ox wagons and 21 French wagons. One wagon carried nothing but the firearms Sir George used — 75 rifles, numerous pistols and a dozen shotguns — to kill 105 bears, and some 2,000 buffalo and elk, and 1,600 deer. He must have found plentiful game because he also evidenced a disinclination to "hunt" for it. He apparently got into a comfortable position for his shots and was then handed a gun by an attendant, who also had to reload Sir George's weapons.

Today some 450 licensed outfitters practice in the state, many of them part-time and some as full-time operators. As a business, it contributes more than $100 million to the Montana economy and even though the industry is going through a period of adjustment to changing conditions it has remained fairly stable for the past decade.

The outfitted hunt serves a distinct need in the hunting fraternity. Many individuals have neither the time nor inclination to "do it on their own" and consequently hire the services of an outfitter to provide them a base

Photo courtesy Steve Copenhaver

Steve Copenhaver leads a string of horses back to camp in the Scapegoat Wilderness after packing out an elk one of his hunters had taken.

of operations. Most often that service also includes a guide, usually one per two hunters, to provide on-the-ground assistance.

A major factor has been success, too. But while the taking of game isn't guaranteed with an outfitter, statistics do show that a higher percentage of hunters who go afield with a professional guide get their game than those who do not.

Several explanations have been given for this, but basically there are two. One, outfitters generally put their clients in high possibility areas. Two, the outfitted hunter usually spends as much as 10 successive days in the field. This is a tremendous advantage over those who have to hunt weekends or who can never get more than two or three days in a row to hunt.

"Time is the vital ingredient. The right time, right place and enough time is never more true than with hunting," hunting consultant Jack Atcheson Sr. of Butte said.

That time exacts a price. Costs vary from outfitter to outfitter, but the going rate at present seems to run from $150 to $250 per day for the hunter who goes afield with one guide and $100 to $200 per day per person for two hunters per guide. To those costs the hunter must add license fees, transportation costs, and the processing and shipment of meat and hides, taxidermy and other extras.

The payoff, however, comes with the quality of the hunt and Montana is one state that has tried in recent years to upgrade the quality of its outfitted services. Outfitters are licensed in Montana and while officials admit that some bad operators need to be weeded out, the majority deliver the services they advertise.

What does one do to select a good, reputable guide?

Outfitter Jack Wemple of Victor, who has been active for many years to upgrade outfitting standards in Montana, suggests that hunters use three basic safeguards in the attempt to locate a good outfitter. They are: 1. Check with either the Montana Department of Fish, Wildlife and Parks or the Montana Outfitters and Guides Association to be sure the outfitter is licensed and reputable; 2. Require references and check them closely by writing or phoning, and 3. Check with people you know who have hunted with outfitters.

Bill Maloit, supervisor of outfitting for the MDFW&P, suggests that hunters always check with his agency or the Montana Outfitters and Guides Association (see addresses in Appendix) as well as the Montana Outfitters Council, an appointive body responsible for administering state law on outfitting. In addition, the outfitters' group publishes an annual booklet that is available free by writing them. The booklet describes services their members provide and also contains a "Sportsman's Alert" that was jointly issued by the Montana Outfitters Council, the Montana Department of Fish, Wildlife and Parks, and the North American Outfitters, Inc. It reads, in part:

"We strongly recommend that before you book, pay or send any fee or deposit to any person (guide or outfitter) that you contact the wildlife agency or other appropriate agencies in the state of interest in order to determine if the person is legally licensed to provided solicited services."

What should an outfitter provide? And what is expected of the hunter-client, since both the outfitter and the hunter contribute to the success of the hunting experience? Maloit, who by his official status is in the middle of such situations, gives advice that cuts both ways: have a written contract made between the parties.

"That eliminates guesswork and confusion, or false expectations," Maloit said. "The hunter knows what the outfitter is to provide, what and where they will hunt, and whether horses will be provided to hunt, and so on."

Maloit noted that only 20 complaints regarding outfitted services came in during the 1984 season, a tiny percentage when considered in terms of the number of hunters who use outfitters. Even so, each complaint is treated seriously, not only because it is important to the individual involved but to the ultimate well-being of the outfitting industry.

The Montana Outfitters and Guides Association has adopted a "Code of Ethics" that is exemplary of what should be expected of outfitters. In shortened form, it provides that the outfitter will:

1. Abide by all applicable conservation and game laws, statutes and

A sure sign of a good hunt is meat hanging in camp. The elk hunting obviously was good for the individuals hunting out of this camp in the Montana wilderness. The protective bags keep the elk quarters clean and also prevent flies and other troublesome insects from contaminating the meat.

regulations and will not condone their violation.

2. Maintain serviceable equipment and gear in good working condition, provide well-cared-for stock, and well-trained and courteous employees.

3. Maintain a neat and orderly and sanitary camp, provide good meals.

4. Clearly define to prospective clients rates, accommodations and services prior to booking and acceptance of down payment.

5. Honestly advise clients of game and fish populations in the area and their chances of encountering the species they desire in the time allocated to the hunt.

6. Advise clients of conditions of weather, terrain, equipment, travel and housing, and equipment and gear they will need, as well as the degree of physical conditioning necessary to fulfill their portion of the agreement.

7. Never fill a client's game bag or bag limit for him or her.

8. Barring unforeseen conditions, as per agreement with the client, all trophies, meat, hides and capes will be prepared and delivered to the processor, taxidermist, or to the client, in a satisfactory and usable condition.

9. Work closely with private landowners, public land management agencies and/or stockmen and respect their rights and privileges.

10. Make every responsible effort to provide for the safety of clients and personnel, including firearms safety.

"Good outfitters have four basic characteristics," Maloit said. "They are preparedness, patience, fortitude and integrity."

Outfitter Len Kopec put father and son Bob (center) and Rich Spencer of California onto these nice mule deer bucks and a bull elk during their outfitted hunt in the Paradise Valley south of Livingston. Kopec is typical of Montana outfitters who provide hunting for both deer and elk.

He explained that preparedness deals with having equipment in good repair and the camp packed in before the hunt, wood cut and everything in order to provide good conditions for the clients. Patience involves dealing with people, stock and weather, fortitude in achieving the best an outfitter can in terms of dealing with resource managers.

"Integrity involves giving the client a quality experience," Maloit said. "That means not being oversold, overbooked, unprepared, providing inexperienced guides, or issuing unethical promises."

Still, no formal or binding code of ethics exists for hunters or clients, and outfitters and administrators agreed that the relationship between outfitters and their clients comes down to their basic two-way relationship.

Maloit believes most problems come from unrealistic expectations brought to the hunt by the clients. "Some of them really expect to find a six-point bull elk behind every tree, and when they don't get anything they get upset," Maloit said. Wemple suggested that the biggest failing involves the hunter-client who comes unprepared for what they encounter on the hunt.

"Physical conditioning is the main problem. Many can't do the strenuous work necessary to hunt in mountain country, some have done nothing to develop their ability with the rifle, and many others simply don't read the advice outfitters provide them in their mail-outs," Wemple said.

Vernon J. Boose (top photo) of Reamstown, Pa., sits astride a large-bodied 5x6 bull elk taken in the Montana wilderness while on an outfitted hunt. Howard Copenhaver, (left) one of the deans of Montana outfitters, and his son Steve secure the elk's quarters on pack animals for their transport out of the mountains.

Mountain mule deer like this one taken by Glen Cousins of Lebanon, Pa., high in the forested terrain of the Scapegoat Wilderness are the second most prized and the most commonly taken big game animal in Montana.

Outfitter Len Kopec outlined another problem outfitters simply can't control and yet one which often leads to a few tense days in camp: that of a hunter who "wants" a trophy but instead shoots the first buck deer or bull elk he comes across and then blames the outfitter for not getting him a bigger animal.

"The hardest thing is getting people to wait, to see if they can get something bigger," Kopec said. "People who want trophies have to learn to wait, and generally hunters tend to get discouraged if it takes them more than a couple of days to get a shot at a trophy animal. What they've got to realize is that some resident hunters hunt five to eight years without getting an elk, let alone a big one."

Kopec is a man who knows wildlife and in many ways is typical of the younger generation of outfitters on the Montana scene. He holds a Master's Degree in Wildlife Biology from the University of Montana and he blends his love of the outdoors with his technical training to provide sound biological advice mixed with a savvy understanding of the art of hunting. He runs a no-nonsense operation and expresses frustration at dealing with unrealistic expectations. As an example, he cited a common expectation — that of a hunter who demands a mule deer with a 30-inch-plus spread. "People have to realize that in Montana there aren't a lot of 30-inch mule deer, period, and further that a deer doesn't have to have

30-inch-plus horns to be a good trophy. We take a lot of trophy mule deer in our area every fall, but precious few that big and outfitters and hunters have to work together so they're dealing with reality."

The emphasis given the two-way relationship has led, in addition to the rules governing outfitters, to a 10-point set of standards for guests. It suggests they:

1. Travel well and get along with the rest of the party.

2. Use care with outfitter's equipment and stock.

3. Practice safety and do not sight in guns at camp or in the hunting area.

4. Realize that alcohol used in moderation is a social privilege.

5. Carefully extinguish cigarettes and matches if they smoke and do not litter trails and countryside.

6. Remember, gun safety is a must and identifying game avoids accident or waste.

7. Display a willingness and the ability to make the stalk and kill.

8. Respect the outfitter's or guide's knowledge of the country and the game habits of the area.

9. Respect the outfitter's requirements for deposit and cancellation deadline.

10. Be responsible for killing and properly tagging their own game.

Obviously, the thrust of both codes is the total hunting experience — the fair chase for game and the relationship among all the people involved. These factors combine to give a hunting experience meaning, and that isn't to diminish the significance of taking game. The point is that killing an elk, deer, antelope, goat or other animal isn't always necessary to have had a successful hunt.

Outfitter-consultant Atcheson put it well: "Based on the average physically-fit client who completes a normal hunt of usual duration, we normally consider success a client who is satisfied that everybody has done their best under the circumstances...What could be more fair?"

Chapter 13

Gear and Equipment

In October of 1984, I joined five hunters from the Missoula area for a deer and antelope hunt in the Missouri Breaks country. Four of us drove out on a Friday morning into the face of a building storm. We carried all our gear in a van and pulled a trailer in which to bring home our game. The other two hunters were to follow the next day with a four-wheel drive pickup.

Unfortunately, that early fall storm worsened, becoming a snowstorm and then a blizzard. Snow piled up and the temperature plummeted. The wind blew steadily at 20-30 miles an hour and gusted to 50. Mountain passes were closed. Travel advisories were issued and already-difficult driving conditions became extremely hazardous. And that was just on the highways. Our companions, even with their four-wheel drive, were unable to join us.

Out in the breaks country, the storm alternated between wind-driven rain and bone-chilling snow. Within hours the usually dry country had become a slick, gumbo-mud nightmare. We simply couldn't get around in in our two-wheel drive and the storm prevented our companions with the four-wheel truck from getting across the mountains and driving the 350 miles to the place we were to hunt. Suddenly, a trip for which we'd planned carefully was ruined. Because of conditions beyond our control, we were undergeared. To move about the rugged breaks country, which required driving some distance from the campsite to the areas we could hunt on private land, a four-wheel drive was absolutely essential under the circumstances. And while we had one, it was 350 miles away and of no use to us at all.

One of the best places in Montana to hunt is the fringe areas where timbered slopes and draws adjoin open grassland. Here a hunter uses a spotting scope in open country to get a fix on mule deer feeding at the edge of the timber at the left.

That, of course, was the ruination of that hunting trip because we had only the weekend for hunting and couldn't wait the storm out — but it wasn't the end of hunting for us. It just simply put an end to **that** hunt and served as a reminder that even the best-planned hunts can be ruined by inadequate or faulty gear.

Sometimes everything we do to properly equip a hunt isn't enough, particularly in places like Montana where the weather can be an overriding factor. But there is no denying that most situations can be handled if you have the proper gear with you — and that applies both to the doing, where some things are simply helpful, and safety, where some things are essential when unforeseen circumstances can threaten your life.

Gearing up for a hunt has its basics, its necessities and its luxuries. And the sort of hunt we go on often decides the category under which we list our "hunting equipment."

For example, a backpack trip several miles from a road might limit us to one extra pair of socks or underclothing while we could take several changes with us if we were camped close to a vehicle or with an outfitter. And while such things are "basics" in certain circumstances, they become a luxury under others. Another example is a tent. I list a good, sturdy ripstop nylon mountain tent capable of handling me and my gear a necessity on all backpack or horsepack hunting trips into the mountains. I've been caught in so many vicious mountain storms that I consider that item essential to survival under such conditions and I'm willing to pay the price of carrying it, whatever the weight. Not only does it give shelter, but because you and your things can be kept dry, you get better rest at night and thereby have more energy to expend during the next day's hunting.

The other side of the coin is to be overgeared, so burdened with excess equipment and gadgets that you can't really exercise the freedom of movement and quickness of travel that hunting often requires. I do this a lot, particularly when packing my pickup or van for an extended hunting trip. The result is that even though I have most of the things I might need with me, I end up fighting my way around equipment in the vehicle, in camp, and on the way home when space is at a premium because the load to be hauled is bigger when game is taken.

Just what is required? First, your basic gear is something only you can determine — a good vehicle, preferably a four-wheel drive — is essential. A quality camper or RV, tent or other shelter is needed if you plan to stay out for any length of time. Campstoves, both for cooking and for heating, lanterns and flashlights, a quality sleeping bag and mattress, water containers, cooking paraphernalia, a sharp axe, some sort of a saw for wood-cutting, toiletry items, a first-aid kit, foul-weather gear, extra clothing, etc.

Outfitted hunts require a different list and most often when you book a hunt with an outfitter, he'll provide you a list of the items he recommends. Pay attention to those recommendations. Conditions vary from location to location and time of year and most outfitters have a good idea of what you'll need under the varying circumstances to be encountered.

Generally, though, the list of basics is universal. Here's a couple provided by two highly regarded Montana's outfitters, one of whom works a camp in the wilderness as well as one at his ranch, and another who has a combination horsepack/four-wheel-drive camp a few miles off the main highway:

Outfitter Jack Wemple: A good sleeping bag (down-filled preferred), warm underclothing and plenty of socks, both wool and lightweight, toilet kit and personal items, rainsuit (two-piece preferred, not a poncho as a poncho can hang up on your saddle and spook your horse), wet weather boots and leather hiking boots (packs are good for wet and cold weather. Vibram soles are best for hunting in this mountain country. A smooth sole boot is best for riding horses, something with a heel on it as a cowboy boot), comfortable shoes for around camp or the lodge, wool pants and shirts, both lightweight and heavy, depending on whether you are hunting early or late season (We recommend wool for hunting as it is quite warm, plus wool will shed a lot of water before you will get wet. Do not wear down vests or jackets when hunting elk and deer.), comfortable jeans, shirts or jackets for around camp, rifle scabbard to fit your rifle, fishing rod, fishing tackle, two boxes of ammo should be sufficient and we will check your rifles at our range at the ranch prior to the day of the hunt, fanny pack or small day pack is nice to carry your camera, lunch and

The use of a tarp-covered lean-to to keep camp equipment under cover is helpful in a mountain camp where storms can move in at a moment's notice. Here's a view taken on successive mornings, one in fair weather and the other a ground-hugging, cloud-shrouded rain that didn't let up for three days.

small items during the day, a side zipper duffel bag is best to pack your gear in as it is easily accessible, and a hunter orange vest of at least 400 square inches is required in Montana.

Outfitter Len Kopec: License and tags, rifle (recommend .270 or larger), ammunition (40 rounds), leather boots with lug soles, rubber-bottomed insulated boots, comfortable shoes or slippers, waterproofing compound for boots, 3-4 pairs of wool socks, cotton socks, long underwear (2 tops, 2 pants), undershirts and shorts, lightweight wool pants, heavy wool pants, flannel or wool shirts, hooded sweatshirt, down vest, wool jacket (medium or heavy-weight), wool gloves, wool mittens, wool stocking cap or hat with ear flaps, blaze orange vest (required in Montana), raingear, pocket knife or sheath knife, shotgun and ammo (optional), fishing gear (optional), camera and film, binoculars (7 or 8 power), compass, waterproof match case, sleeping bag, sleeping pad (cots are provided), flashlight, day pack or belt pack, towels, toiletry articles, personal medication, extra eyeglasses or contacts.

"Whatever you do, don't hunt in Montana wearing an insulated coverall type suit," Len Kopec said. "You'll end up wet, either by sweating because it's too warm or soaked and chilled once you get into snow and the suit gets wet. They're next to worthless when wet, and they take a long time to dry. Wear wool."

Outfitters also emphasize physical conditioning. To whatever degree

you're able, get yourself into sufficient condition to withstand the rigors of climbing several thousand feet of elevation per day while making awesome expenditures of physical energy. And then limit yourself to what you're realistically capable of doing.

Smoke Elser of Missoula, who is one of the more knowledgeable outfitters I've encountered, encourages his hunters to spend a lot of time conditioning before they come. He's seen too many hunts ruined because the hunter came into camp unprepared for the conditions always present on a mountain hunt. Simply put, it's a physically demanding activity even when horses are used to accomplish most of your travel in the mountains.

Another of the common "gear" problems involves the feet — new boots that haven't been broken in or feet that haven't been toughened up to the boots. As one who is as guilty as anyone in regard to this, let me tell you that pushing yourself out on a steep hillside day after day when you're fighting open blisters caused by new boots is not the right way to go. I know. It happened to me one year when a pair of my old faithfuls literally came apart during the first week of hunting season. I'd trusted those old boots too long and paid the price with considerable agony when I had to get and break in new boots right during the season. It was a good but painful lesson.

Bob Miller of the Montana Department of Fish, Wildlife and Parks is an expert in survival basics. He recommends you begin with the feet by always selecting the right sort of footgear for what you're doing. I'm partial to Vibram soles in the mountains and I have them on both my leather boots for hunting when there is no snow and my leather-top, rubber-bottomed packs for hunting in snow. In the warmer weather of archery boots for hunting, when there is no snow and my leather-topped, rubber-bottomed packs for hunting in snow. In the warmer weather of achery

A pair of sturdy leather boots are essential for hunting in much of Montana where the bothersome prickly pear cactus can penetrate light leather and occasionally even the sides of fairly heavy boots. Foot placement is carefully done when hunting where this plant is found.

season, I often wear sturdy "sneaker" type shoes to enable quieter movement, but if the weather turns, I shift to my sturdier leather boots in an instant. You've got to protect your feet to keep yourself able to hunt day after day.

Miller advises the hunter to gear up for his or her personal needs by simply considering the needs of the body — which basically are to have water and food to supply energy and clothing to keep warm.

He starts with foot gear and moves on to the right combination of clothing to maintain body heat. "Use the 'layering' system," he said. "Consider the type of underwear which ventilates or 'breathes.' The second layer should provide comfort, utility and durability — wool pants and wool shirts work well. Carry an outer garment that is waterproof and windproof should inclement weather occur unexpectedly. Covering your head is especially important because a great deal of body heat is lost when you are bareheaded."

Clothing is important because the biggest killer in the outdoors is a thing called "hypothermia." A condition similar to a fever except that it is in reverse, hypothermia occurs when your body temperature drops a few degrees. It is caused by exposure to cold and is aggravated by wet clothes, wind and exhaustion. It is a rapid and progressive mental and physical collapse, which accompanies the chilling of the inner core of the body — and it can be fatal. Early symptoms are uncontrolled shivering, memory lapses, numbness, vague, slow speech, fumbling hands and frequent stumbling. Without treatment, stupor, collapse and ultimately death can follow. EVERY HUNTER WHO GOES AFIELD IN MONTANA FACES THE POSSIBILITY OF HYPOTHERMIA IF HE OR SHE ISN'T PROPERLY PREPARED.

The best way to prevent hypothermia is to avoid exposure and stay dry. But that isn't always possible, so like many safety officials, Miller recommends that you wear the kind of clothing that retains its insulating qualities when wet. Wool is an excellent example. Cotton isn't, nor is down. Both lose about 90 percent of their insulating value if they become wet and once your wetness is combined with the other two great causes of hypothermia, low temperatures and wind, watch out! Wind multiplies your problems because its chill factor can quickly carry you beyond the threshhold of your body to cope with the cold.

"If you can't get back to camp or to your vehicle, concentrate on finding shelter and building a fire," Miller said. "A shelter may be constructed of lumber, bark, paper, cardboard, plastic, snow, dirt, or it can be as simple as a bushel-sized plastic garbage bag. In emergencies such as unexpected wind, rain or snowstorms where shelter is mandatory, do what wildlife does — crawl under or burrow into foliage."

Now that's good advice, but lots and lots of times I've been in open breaks and prairie country or high, open tundra in the mountains where there simply was no shelter to be had until I got to camp or a vehicle. I've discussed this situation often with outfitters and other hunters experienced in being out under Montana hunting conditions and the consensus seems to be that the best thing to do is to try to never extend yourself to the point that you can't get out if you get in trouble. In other words, don't take chances — and if you do get into trouble, provide for your bodily safety and survival **before** you get so weakened you can't.

Safety official Miller provided a list of eight things that will help hunters in Montana gear up for potential survival situations. "Before going hunting, look ahead to what you will need," he said. "Careful advance planning and understanding of your own limitations are just as important as knowing what to do."

Miller was speaking about the problem of getting lost, but his advice applies as well to other critical, life-threatening situations. Here are his eight points:

1. Choose hunting locations that complement your outdoor proficiency.

2. Always let someone know where you are going.

3. Avoid hazardous terrain.

4. Avoid unreasonable challenges.

5. Be prepared for the type of weather usually associated with the

season, but also be prepared for the unexpected.

6. Choose companions with care. Try to match skill proficiencies as well as physical capabilities. Don't hunt alone.

7. Remember that strenuous exercise will require more energy and will create more stress on both mind and body.

8. Add the word S-T-O-P to your hunting lingo. When you don't know exactly where you are or you encounter an emergency situation: S = stop and sit down; T = think; O = observe; and P = plan.   Also, use your survival kit as needed.

Minimal Survival Kit

1. One foot of heavy, cotton string dipped in melted paraffin and wrapped in wax paper. A short, frayed piece of this burns longer and hotter than a match.

2. Salt in a foil packet. This could improve the flavor of anything caught and cooked for food.

3. Two snelled fish hooks and a small amount of fishing line.

4. Black electrician's tape that can be used to fasten splints and repair torn clothing.

5. A snare. Picture-hanging wire works well for this purpose.

6. Steel wool (00 and finer) makes excellent tinder.

7. Water purification tablets should be carried and used whenever there is any doubt about the purity of drinking water.

8. A small tube of antibiotic ointment for cuts and burns.

9. Wooden matches should be dipped in paraffin to make them waterproof.

10. Safety pins can be used to replace buttons or hold torn clothing together.

11. Emergency food. Several packets of condensed soup mix and other items that can be easily prepared and eaten.

12. A small whistle. This is used to blast distress calls. Three blasts are recognized as a distress signal.

13. Adhesive bandages.

14. A general purpose knife.

15. Nylon rope or plastic binder twine. Excellent for tying together a makeshift camp.

16. A space blanket.

17. A flashlight. I usually include one in my regular gear.

18. A wire saw is a handy item.

19. Survival booklet.

20. Candle.

21. Compass and topographic map. If you don't have a sense for the lay of the land, these are essential items.

22. The container you carry the above items in should have a mirror glued into the lid for use as a signal to search aircraft.

Chapter 14

Safety

Accidents are a part of any human activity, including hunting. But so is the other side of the tragedy coin, carelessness. Many incidents involving injury and even death can be, or could have been, prevented. At the risk of sounding preachy, it's worth reminding you that your safety and the safety of those around you depends directly on you.

For years I worked on a newspaper news desk; among other things it was my job to cover stories involving hunting accidents. I reported far too many of them and came to realize that there are two basic aspects to most accidents. First, as is always the case when an element of risk is involved in any activity, some people were injured in true accidents — a slip on the mountain, a horse stumbling or throwing a rider, a knife or axe cut, a tree falling on a campsite, etc. The vast majority of accidents, however, involve a common denominator that can be eliminated — and that is human carelessness, either of preparation or in the act of handling dangerous equipment or participating in hunting-related activities.

Second, I guess I'm a coward regarding hunting hazards even though I know I take many calculated risks in the mountains. It's simply that there's an awful lot of difference between doing something that's careless and doing something under conditions where you can assess the risk involved and minimize it.

There are two reasons for my personal attitude, which admittedly borders on the fanatic, regarding safety — particularly with firearms. When I was 15 one of my high school buddies was killed when he shot himself with his carbine, while sitting in a pickup truck. He made two

A river ford on the South Fork of the Flathead River. Yes, the river does flow through that narrow gorge in the background and a slip here would carry a horse or foot wader into it. Care must be exercised at every step when wading deeper rivers like this one.

mistakes: he took a loaded gun into a vehicle and he carried it in the cab muzzle up. The gun accidently discharged and he was instantly killed. That incident occurred more than 30 years ago, but I still remember the trauma of that event as vividly as if it were yesterday.

Also seared in my mind is another event that took place about the same time. A hunter new to Montana, who had never seen an elk, went hunting in the South Fork of the Flathead and in the pre-dawn light of opening day fired on an "elk" that was walking up the trail toward him. The problem was, he wasn't shooting at elk. He shot into a string of horses bearing riders into the mountains; he killed two of those riders.

Accidents happen all the time, although they certainly have been reduced from the number that occurred during the terrible times of the 1950s. One reason has been the adoption of safety regulations that are strictly enforced, the most noticeable of which are the requirement of a hunter orange outer garment when a hunter is in the field and hunter safety training and certification for young hunters.

For example, 16 hunting related accidents occurred in 1983 and 14 in 1984. Most involved firearms; and officials in the hunter education division of the Montana Department of Fish, Wildlife and Parks noted that some of the accidents could have been avoided if safe gun handling had been followed. "Many were the result of carelessness," a department report states. One fatal accident occurred each year.

The accident reports give a good idea of the safety factors involved:

- Two persons were injured when a shotgun accidentally fired inside a pickup truck. The 12-gauge shotgun had been placed between the two passengers, with the barrel pointed downward.

• As the 13-year-old hunter made his way through a fence, a 30.06 rifle leaning against the fence discharged and the bullet struck a nearby rock. The victim's legs were sprayed with shards of rock, but he escaped serious injury.

• The victim's hunting companion was shooting at a deer, did not know his partner was on the other side of it, and accidentally shot him.

• The victim was resting his rifle, barrel down on his right foot, playing with the safety when the gun discharged. The victim lost his middle toe.

• Upon exiting the back of a pickup truck, the butt of the youngster's rifle struck the vehicle. The rifle discharged, hitting and killing the boy's companion.

• Two hunters were riding in a pickup truck when it struck a snowbank. The impact knocked two rifles out of a gun rack, causing one to discharge. The victim was hit in the shoulder.

• While walking down a hill, the hunter slipped and fell. His .22 revolver discharged through his leg.

• The victim was struck by a high-powered rifle bullet. The bullet also struck the breech of her gun, causing it to explode into shrapnel, which caused further injury. The shooter left the scene.

• A hunter mistook a pet dog carrying a blue pack for a wolf and shot the creature while its owner was several feet away.

• Two men were shooting gophers. One of them shot in the direction of the victim, who received a superficial wound.

And so it goes, from season to season and on and on. Each year some of the accidents are self inflicted and each year people are victimized by other hunters' carelessness, as was the woman shot by the assailant who fled the scene.

Several efforts have been made to improve hunters' knowledge of firearm and field safety and most accidents do involve firearms. One of the best such efforts are hunter safety programs like the Montana Hunter Education Program, which in 1984 received the highest rating (AAA) given for such programs by the International Association of Fish and Wildlife Agencies.

Such recognition is the result of an extremely successful program designed to put hunters in the field who not only know but practice safe firearm principles. The program began in Montana in 1958 and since then more than 186,000 youngsters and numerous adults have completed the training. Montana law requires anyone between the ages of 12 and 18 to pass the hunter education course prior to purchasing a hunting license.

Courses are taught by approximately 650 volunteers across the state. Those interested in taking it should contact their local sportsman's organization or the offices of the Montana Department of Fish, Wildlife and Parks. Instructors must spend a minimum of 10 hours teaching their classes such things as firearm safety, hunter responsibility, wildlife conservation, survival and much more.

Montana officials credit their volunteer instructors for their AAA rating. "These men and women are the heart of the program and without their devotion, the program would not be the success it is," a department spokesman said.

Among the major things they teach are the *Ten Commandments of of Firearm Safety* and the National Rifle Association's code of hunter's ethics.

Ten Commandments of Firearm Safety

1. Treat every gun with the respect due a loaded gun.

2. Watch that muzzle! Be able to control the direction of the muzzle even if you should stumble.

3. Be sure the barrel and action are clear of obstructions and that you have only ammunition of the proper size for the gun you are carrying.

4. Be sure of your target before you pull the trigger; know identifying features of the game you hunt.

5. Unload guns when not in use. Take down or have actions open; guns should be carried in cases to the shooting area.

6. Never point a gun at anything you do not want to shoot; avoid all horseplay with a firearm.

7. Never climb a fence or tree or jump a ditch with a loaded gun; never pull a gun toward you by the muzzle.

8. Never shoot a bullet at a flat, hard surface or water; at target practice be sure your backstop is adequate.

9. Store guns and ammunition separately beyond the reach of children and careless adults.

10. Avoid alcoholic beverages before or during shooting.

Another helpful list of safety recommendations come from the National Rifle Association, which carries the safety theme beyond to the notion of hunter responsibility in other areas as well:

NRA's Hunter's Code of Ethics

1. I will consider myself an invited guest of the landowner, seeking his permission and so conducting myself that I may be welcome in the future.

2. I will obey the rules of safe gun handling and will courteously but firmly insist that others who hunt with me do the same.

3. I will obey all game laws and regulations and will insist that my companions do likewise.

4. I will do my best to acquire those marksmanship and hunting skills which assure clean, sportsmanlike kills.

5. I will support conservation efforts which can assure good hunting for future generations of Americans.

6. I will pass along to younger hunters the attitudes and skills essential to a true outdoor sportsman.

And good hunting, too!

Chapter 15

Rules and Regulations

In 1984 I was called as a resident of my Montana county to serve on a jury in court proceedings. To my surprise, a hunting violation was involved. A man had been charged with spotlighting big game at night on a ranch in the Bitterroot Valley — and his major line of defense was that he hadn't known it was against the law. Yes, he said, he had once seen a copy of the regulations handed out free to all hunters when they purchase their licenses, but he hadn't thought it important to read them through. And since he didn't know that it was illegal to be on someone else's property at night, or that it was illegal to flash a spotlight from a motor vehicle in which a gun was carried, he said he should be found innocent of the charge.

There were several hunters on that jury; each of us was as appalled at the individual's attitude as we were his sorry story. We, the jury, found him guilty, a point insignificant to our purpose here but indicative of a general attitude among the vast majority of hunters I've been around. To wit, most hunters detest poachers and habitual game law violaters and almost all hunters make a serious effort to obey game laws.

Some people do purposely violate game laws. Many infractions, however, occur accidentally or inadvertently. Regulations change and people don't know it or they haven't bothered to inform themselves. Good intentions and lack of knowledge, however, aren't acceptable defenses — so it's best for all hunters to realize the reasons behind the do's and don'ts of hunting regulations.

Regulations are intended to do four things: 1. Assure each hunter an

A freshly-fallen snow blankets the Bitterroot Mountains as this hunter contemplates a day-long outing into excellent elk and mule deer country.

equal opportunity to take game; 2. Provide an adequate harvest of game; 3. Protect private and public property; and 4. Provide for public safety.

There were 4,575 violations cited in 1983, the last year for which figures are available. The majority of these were for two reasons, fishing without a license and, of significance to hunters, hunting big game without landowner permission.

This latter point is interesting. A year earlier, state enforcement personnel had indicated that tagging big game animals — which is required immediately following the kill — was the number one problem of big game hunters. Other violations included failure to wear an outer garment of at least 400 inches of fluorescent hunter orange material and hunting big game without landowner permission. The last violation is today's number one problem.

One word of caution, particularly regarding the oft-cited tagging of game animals. State wardens are instructed to be sticklers for details on this hunter responsibility, which is to completely cut out the day and month on which the kill took place. Merely slitting the proper day and month or marking them with a pen will not suffice. And once the tag is validated, it must be attached to the game at the site of the kill, not after the animal has been dragged or carried back to a vehicle or camp. Then the validated tag should always remain with the animal carcass (meat) even if the horns or antlers are removed. The the tag must stay attached to the carcass or with the meat of the animal as long as any portion of the animal remains unconsumed. Why? Because the tagging process is the one way of ensuring that a hunter does not take more than the allowable limit of one game animal for each tag.

Another caution: a new law brought about by the need to provide finer tuning of management from district to district involves the requirement that evidence of sex be attached to big game animals. Many hunters have run afoul of this regulation and they might as well get used to following it. So long as we enjoy expanded either-sex seasons in neighboring districts, evidence of sex will be required.

Erv Kent, administrator of the Law Enforcement Division for the Department of Fish, Wildlife and Parks, suggests that the best method of determining an animal's sex and species is to leave the animal's head attached. If this is impossible or a hunter takes an antlerless deer or elk, or a doe or fawn antelope, and wraps the animal's carcass in sheets or places it in a cheese-cloth bag, another type of evidence of sex, such as the udder, must remain attached.

Kent said the agency has had to develop special tactics to meet overall enforcement problems simply because of geography. With 147,138 square miles to cover, Kent's officers are constantly afield to check for poaching, licenses, etc. But they've also instituted a couple of measures intended to have a preventive effect on would-be violators. They are basically an undercover approach — sending out-of-uniform wardens into areas where they're not known, and special "saturation teams" where agency personnel are concentrated at a special location.

The latter tactic, for example, worked to perfection during one recent season when the team caught redhanded a group of hunters who'd set up camp in an isolated part of southwestern Montana the week before season and had a load of deer and elk ready to leave the state on the afternoon of the first day of hunting season. Instead, the enforcement team, acting on a tip from a hunter who'd encountered the party and its illegal activities the year before, concentrated their efforts, located and arrested the gang of poachers.

Regulations of significance include:

Access
Leased state lands may be posted against trespass by the lessee. Private landowners are not required to provide access to state lands that are accessible only across private property.

Caliber
There are no caliber limitations. It is prohibited to use any poisonous, explosive, or deleterious substances on or in any arrowheads, bullet, or projectile. It is prohibited to use a shotgun to shoot deer except with loads of 0 buck, 00 buck or single ball loads.

Checking Stations
Hunters and fishermen are required to stop at checking stations on their routes of travel to and from hunting and fishing areas. Vital hunting and harvest information is gathered at checking stations.

Clothing Color

With the exception of archers during special archery seasons, it shall be unlawful for any person to hunt big game animals or to accompany any hunter as an outfitter or guide without wearing exterior garments above the waist totaling not less than 400 square inches of hunter orange material, visible at all times while hunting.

Evidence of Sex and Species

Hunters taking big game must leave evidence of sex and species attached to the carcass. In addition, hunters taking elk or deer during antlered only seasons must be able to show on demand for inspection the complete head and antlers.

Evidence of sex must be left attached to the carcass of a big game animal until the carcass is processed (cut up). The game tag must remain with the processed meat.

The evidence of sex requirement is met when the head, horns or antlers are left naturally attached to the whole carcass or a front quarter. If the head is removed, some other external evidence of sex (either scrotum, penis, testicles for male animals, or udder for female animals) must remain.

Game Limits

Unless otherwise specified, the limit of big game for each license year shall be one of each species of big game, subject to sex and age specifications as designated on regulations.

Game Tags

When you have killed your game animals, cut out the proper month and day from the carcass tag and immediately attach the tag to the carcass so it remains visible at all times.

Game Parts Suitable for Food

Montana state law prohibits the waste of any part of any game animal, game bird, or game fish suitable for food. Following are guidelines as to parts "suitable for food."

Big Game : All of the four quarters above the hock including loin and backstrap. (Black bear, grizzly bear and mountain lions are excluded by law.)

Game Birds : Only the breasts must be retained from all birds that fall into the size category of the partridge or smaller.

Breasts and thighs must be retained from all birds larger than a partridge up to the size category of pheasants and sage grouse.

Breasts, thighs and wings must be retained from all birds larger than pheasants or sage grouse.

Migratory Waterfowl : Only the breasts must be retained from all birds that fall into the size category of a teal duck or smaller.

Breasts and thighs must be retained from all birds larger than a teal duck up to the size category of a mallard duck.

Breasts, thighs and wings must be retained from all birds larger than mallard ducks.

Hunting Districts

The state has been divided into legally described hunting districts designated by numbers, wherein the limits, season dates, species and sex of game animals which may be taken are specified. These districts are as shown on the official annual hunting map issued by the Montana Department of Fish, Wildlife and Parks. The map defines districts in which deer, elk, bear, mountain lion, antelope, moose, bighorn sheep and mountain goat hunting are permitted and another document entitled "Legal Descriptions" gives more specific descriptions of the districts. These documents are available at Fish, Wildlife and Parks offices and from agents that sell hunting and fishing licenses.

Hunting Hours

Authorized periods small be from one-half hour before sunrise until one-half hour after sunset each day of the hunting season.

Importation of Horses and Mules

The Montana Department of Livestock requires an animal health permit prior to entry. For information call 406-444-2043. A brand inspection is required within Montana.

Littering

A person convicted of littering while hunting, fishing, camping or trapping shall forfeit his license or privileges to hunt, fish, camp or trap within Montana for a period of one year.

Marked Animals

Hunters may encounter big game animals that have radio collars, neck bands or markers. It is legal to shoot such animals, but markers and radios must be returned to the Department of Fish, Wildlife and Parks.

Permission to Hunt

Montana law requires that big game hunters must obtain permission of the landowners, lessees or their agents before hunting big game animals on private property.

Unlawful Activities

It is unlawful in Montana to:

Bait bears.

Waste any part of a game animal suitable for food excepting bears and mountain lions.

Hunt or take any game animal without having a valid license on your person.

While hunting game to act in a negligent manner or knowingly fail to give all reasonable assistance to any person whom you have injured.

Transfer your license or use any license or tag issued to another person.

Shoot game animals on or from any public highway.

Shoot a game animal for someone else's tag.

Shoot or attempt to shoot game animals with the aid of artificial light.

Shoot game animals or birds from an automobile or other self-propelled vehicle.

Use firearms or create any other unlawful disturbance in any game preserve created by the state legislature or Fish and Game Commission.

Hire or retain any unlicensed outfitter or guide.

Cast a spotlight from a motor vehicle when in possession of a firearm or other implement capable of killing wildlife or domestic animals (landowners are excepted).

Use a self-propelled vehicle to concentrate, drive, rally, stir up or harass game, or furbearing animals.

Resident Licenses

License requirements change from year to year and hunters are advised to check annually for such changes.

Basic residency requirements are that anyone applying for a resident Montana hunting license must be a legal resident of Montana for a period of six months immediately prior to making application.

In addition, residents under the age of 18 years are required to present a **Montana** Certificate of Competency to their license agent before being issued a hunting license.

Persons applying for drawings must be at least 12 years of age prior to Sept. 15 of the season for which application is being made, and they must have completed the required firearms safety training course if under 18.

Nonresident Licenses

A Wildlife Conservation License is required before other licenses may be purchased. You may apply for other licenses at the same time you apply for a Conservation License.

Nonresident juveniles under 18 are required to show proof of successfully completing a course in the safe handling of firearms in another state or province before being issued a Montana hunting license. The course must have been completed under the direction of a certified instructor.

Chapter 16

Sportsman's Calendar

January
- Tentative dates for next calendar year's big game seasons are proposed.
- Tentative quotas and bag limits for deer, elk, antelope, moose, sheep, goat, lion, black and grizzly bear for the general season are set.
- Tentative quotas for special deer and elk licenses and permits are set.
- Tentative dates of spring gobbler season proposed by Department of Fish, Wildlife and Parks (DFW&P).
- Commission sets tentative dates of spring gobbler season.

February
- DFW&P conducts public meetings to discuss tentatives. This is the public chance to comment on and alter proposed seasons.
- Mountain lion season closes.
- Mountain lion chase season opens.

March
- New license year begins for big game hunting, bird hunting and fishing.
- Formal hearing on proposed tentative seasons held by Commission.
- Final dates for next calendar year's big game seasons.
- Tentative deer, elk, black and grizzly bear bag limits and harvest quotas for general deer, elk seasons adopted by Commission.
- Spring turkey gobbler season set by Commission.
- Nonresident "A" licenses go on sale.

April
- Nonresident big game combination licenses go on sale.
- Mountain lion chase season closes.
- Spring turkey season usually opens.
- Some spring black bear seasons open.
- All trapping ends.

May
- Tentative dates for upland bird seasons set by Commission.
- General fishing season opens.
- Be sure to mail in applications for special permits.

June
- Deadline for applications for special permits, usually by June 1.
- Final license quotas for moose, sheep and goat.
- Upland game bird season dates set by Commission.
- Tentative trapping season dates and harvest limits set by Commission.

July
- New trapping license year begins.

August
- Final license-permit quotas for antelope, deer and elk.
- Upland game bird seasons set.
- Tentative waterfowl seasons set.
- Aug. 31 is the last day to apply for lion, grizzly and unlimited sheep licenses.
- Drawings conducted for special permits.

September
- Archery seasons open for antelope, deer and elk.
- Upland game bird season gets under way.
- Special backcountry elk and deer hunting opens, usually about mid-month.
- Every other year district boundaries and legal descriptions for the next two year's big game seasons are proposed and finalized.
- Season dates and harvest quotas fur bearers are set by Commission.
- Tentative fishing regulations proposed.
- Waterfowl season generally opens.
- Most moose, sheep, and goat seasons open.

October
- Archery season closes.
- General antelope season opens.
- Big game general season opens.
- Special goat, moose, sheep, deer, elk and grizzly seasons close.
- Pheasant season usually opens.

November
- General antelope season closes.
- General hunting season closes.
- General fishing season closes.
- Most pheasant seasons usually close.
- Nov. 30 last date to get bobcat, lynx and wolverine validation.
- Final fishing regulations for next license year adopted by Commission.

December
- Mountain lion season opens.
- Gallatin-Gardiner late elk hunt usually opens.
- Most waterfowl seasons usually close.
- Most furbearer seasons usually open.

Chapter 17

A Final Word or Two

By now there can be no doubt that hunting in Montana is a mighty big enterprise. It is awesome, not only in potential but in practice. Few, if any, of us will have either the time or energy across a lifetime to pursue it to the limit — though it's been a delight to give it a try over the years.

The ultimate significance of hunting in the Big Sky Country is that while the choices are on a grand scale, the actual doing comes down to the personal level. Each individual undertakes the sport at his or her level of choosing or challenge. From the casual weekend gunner to the confirmed trophy hunter, Montana hunting provides not only a full spectrum of opportunity, but the diversity of geography to accommodate just about any individual's taste or limitations of time and physical capability. Jack Atcheson Sr. was right in declaring that Montana hunting is second to none in terms of the diversity of species hunted.

To that point must be added one I brought up in Chapter 2: Unlike hunting in many places famous for big game species, such as Alaska and Africa, hunting in Montana is readily available to the average person without the necessity of mounting a full-scale expedition. You can easily drive to most points of access. You can hunt on your own, though outfitters are available should you want their services. And, in some parts of the state, you can hunt several big game species at the same time. In most of eastern Montana, for example, you can pursue antelope and deer at the same time. In others you can hunt deer, elk and bear simultaneously and, wherever you're hunting, it is no more than a few hours' drive to move from one part of Montana to another and change your entire hunting

An example of the type of bighorn ram trophies to be found in the Beartooth Mountains. Jack Atcheson Jr. of Butte took this 39x34 bighorn that scored 175 points Boone and Crockett points while guiding another hunter who took a 38-inch ram at the same time. This was the third ram Atcheson has taken in the area in the last 11 years.

situation.

That isn't to suggest that you can flip-flop around the state, willy-nilly, and expect good results. You'll have to do some planning and utilize what daylight hours there are for hunting rather than traveling. Careful planning is essential, particularly for those of us whose jobs require us to squeeze our hunting time into the weekends. Arrangements of access and logistics, not to mention the selection of specific hunting areas, must be taken care of ahead of time because the days are much shorter in the fall. You can't afford to lose a lot of hunting time by being on the highway when you should be in the field. Consequently, most of us hunt within a few hours' drive of our homes. Only occasionally does a more ambitious hunting trip take us several hundred miles away to another part of the state — and that holds true for most people wherever they live in the state.

This brings us to another point I wish to make about hunting in Montana: that of utilizing a resource to its full potential. On one hand, hunting is a tool of wildlife management. It simultaneously provides the use of a resource, in terms of both meat and recreation, and a means of keeping wildlife species from overpopulating their range. On the other hand, there is another dimension that deserves discussion — that of under-utilization of parts of the wildlife resource. In much of Montana we could be taking advantage of hunting opportunities, with no detriment to the resource, that are going untapped today.

Much needs to be done by hunters and their various organizations to work with landowners to improve relationships and open vast tracts of land to hunting that are now closed. This would be to the ultimate benefit of both. Even more can be done to revise our laws and permit systems to provide for expansion of deer seasons in certain areas; whitetail deer provide a tremendous example of one species that is greatly underharvested in many areas.

One more point: those of us who hunt also had better heed the lessons of the past, lessons bitterly learned not only in Montana but elsewhere. Good hunting does not come about by accident. Not only must we remember that what we enjoy today is largely the result of conservation efforts of the past, we must also remember that hunting is a privilege that demands we do it responsibly.

We also had better remember that those of us who hunt must carry the banner for hunting. We are not only the practictioners of the sport but its champions. Most of the things that make for quality hunting in Montana today — such as premium wildlife habitat, large tracts of wilderness, ongoing biological monitoring and landowner-sportsman programs — have come about because hunters committed their time and money and energy to the cause. Tomorrow's hunting opportunities demand the same commitment of us that others gave to provide the incredible opportunities we enjoy today. So we must protect our hunting heritage, you and I, and pass it on, in as good a shape as we found it, to succeeding generations.

Lastly, we must keep our perspective of hunting's role in our lives. The process of hunting actually takes up a small part of the hunter's time — a month or two at the most. That's what makes hunting so special. The rest of the time, those months between hunting seasons when reality is suspended, we think about hunting and talk about hunting and dream about the hunt we want to make next year. We realize that hunting helps shape the way we think about ourselves and the world around us.

Anticipation plays a big role in a hunter's life. So does hope. No matter what took place in previous seasons, we always believe the next hunt is going to be the best ever. That's why anticipation and hope are such powerful motivators. They get us to the top of the next ridge, to seek the challenge of a new mountain, to set goals and pursue them to the fullest, and to share the camaraderie of others who hold the same values. Hope also takes us back into the field after we've failed to take game because hunters tend to be optimistic people — they know that fulfillment comes only occasionally from the bagging of game. Most of the time we're fully satisfied with having made the effort.

In other words, there's sufficient fulfillment to be found in the hunter simply doing his or her thing. When you're out hunting, you're fully alive — physically, mentally and spiritually — and few things in today's world offer that fullness of life. What Montana offers is a setting that more than matches the best of what is to be experienced in hunting. Enough said!

Mike Lindquist of Eureka took this bull elk at 37 yards with a bow in 1984, the second in two years since he seriously took up bowhunting. Note the dense vegetation and his use of camouflage paint on his face.

Chapter 18

Charts of Harvest

The following charts were prepared from statistics provided by the Montana Department of Fish, Wildlife and Parks. They represent trends rather than precise harvests of big game animals.

Antelope

Year	No. Hunters	Harvest	Percent Success
1966	19,556	13,865	71
1967	18,052	12,599	70
1968	16,150	11,500	71
1969	19,871	14,543	73
1970	23,697	18,023	76
1971	24,802	18,403	74
1972	27,762	19,710	71
1973	28,062	19,303	69
1974	27,163	18,810	69
1975	25,022	17,298	69
1976	23,273	16,292	70
1977	24,214	18,528	77
1978	18,393	13,471	73
1979	14,170	10,039	71
1980	16,104	12,016	75
1981	18,973	14,954	79
1982	22,767	20,830	92
1983	32,174	27,485	96
1984	37,007	33,090	89

Black Bear

Year	No. Hunters	Harvest	Percent Success
1966	9,760	2,000	21
1967	10,571	2,130	20
1968	8,290	1,700	24
1969	8,787	1,700	20
1970	7,204	1,079	15
1971	5,105	1,185	23
1972	3,382	928	27
1973	5,019	1,347	27
1974	5,705	1,527	27
1975	6,201	1,252	20
1976	10,187	1,637	16
1977	10,652	1,733	16
1978	5,262	909	17
1979	10,666	795	7
1980	18,135	1,870	10
1981	13,262	1,450	11
1982	10,642	1,277	13
1983	13,062	1,820	14
1984	11,354	1,373	12

Deer

Date	No. Hunters	Harvest	Percent Success
1966	106,180	98,100	92
1967	115,185	88,640	77
1968	125,711	99,250	79
1969	128,177	102,800	80
1970	136,903	110,988	80
1971	141,243	116,716	83
1972	152,545	112,996	74
1973	167,359	137,441	82
1974	154,110	103,656	67
1975	148,109	77,496	52
1976	112,783	43,291	38
1977	120,798	54,143	45
1978	125,054	53,933	43
1979	139,895	64,134	46
1980	151,918	85,164	56
1981	153,710	88,797	58
1982	160,077	100,340	62
1983	203,256	139,467	69
1984	238.036	169,649	71

Elk

Date	No. Hunters	Harvest	Percent Success
1966	55,133	13,400	23
1967	71,883	14,500	21
1968	79,692	16,700	21
1969	73,848	12,100	16
1970	77,819	13,988	18
1971	72,337	11,785	16
1972	75,951	10,867	15
1973	87,746	17,498	20
1974	89,369	10,930	12
1975	91,956	15,750	17
1976	74,190	7,860	11
1977	79,628	13,342	17
1978	86,636	12,017	14
1979	89,367	11,692	13
1980	89,882	14,841	17
1981	88,153	12,868	15
1982	90,103	14,009	16
1983	99,198	17,122	17
1984	86,443	18,478	21

Moose

Date	No. Hunters	Harvest	Percent Success
1966	666	510	74
1967	616	433	70
1968	643	457	71
1969	645	457	71
1970	670	518	86
1971	677	474	70
1972	651	427	66
1973	766	597	78
1974	780	532	68
1975	763	498	65
1976	698	376	54
1977	587	401	68
1978	569	406	71
1979	568	421	74
1980	525	389	74
1981	508	408	80
1982	567	497	88
1983	567	481	85
1984	619	554	89

Mountain Goat

Date	No. Hunters	Harvest	Percent Success
1966	Limited - 459	225	49
	Unlimit - 836	250	30
1967	Limited - 589	294	50
	Unlimit - 256	90	35
1968	Limited - 598	263	44
	Unlimit - 200	29	14
1969	Limited - 537	267	49
	Unlimit - 213	66	31
1970	Limited - 573	303	52
	Unlimit - 223	51	23
1971	Limited - 547	238	44
	Unlimit - 215	59	27
Unlimited discontinued.			
1972	546	234	43
1973	556	280	50
1974	571	306	54
1975	508	237	47
1976	500	302	60
1977	410	230	56
1978	409	238	58
1979	392	234	60
1980	339	230	68
1981	336	208	62
1982	308	170	55
1983	290	189	65
1984	315	215	68

Bighorn Sheep

Date	No. Hunters	Harvest	Percent Success
1966	Limited - 74	44	59
	Unlimit - 281	32	11
1967	Limited - 78	56	73
	Unlimit - 145	12	8
1968	Limited - 75	55	74
	Unlimit - 172	13	7
1969	Limited - 77	50	65
	Unlimit - 279	17	7
1970	Limited - 59	43	73
	Unlimit - 447	31	7
1971	Limited - 64	50	78
	Unlimit - 452	40	9
1972	Limited - 72	50	70
	Unlimit - 574	54	9
1973	Limited - 76	57	75
	Unlimit - 754	35	5
1974	Limited - 98	80	82
	Unlimit - 776	54	7
1975	Limited - 121	89	74
	Unlimit - 631	10	2
1976	Limited - 124	100	81
	Unlimit - 534	20	4
1977	Limited - 90	81	90
	Unlimit - 438	24	5
1978	Limited - 133	113	85
	Unlimit - 510	23	4
1979	Limited - 121	109	91
	Unlimit - 651	34	5
1980	Limited - 181	166	91
	Unlimit - 303	15	5
1981	Limited - 180	164	91
	Unlimit - 384	14	4
1982	Limited - 220	202	92
	Unlimit - 449	18	4
1983	Limited - 351	316	90
	Unlimit - 538	33	6
1984	477	278	58

Archery Hunting — Deer

Year	No. Hunters	Harvest	Percent Success
1968	1,988	275	13.8
1969	1,738	259	14.9
1970	3,438	440	12.7
1971	4,066	593	14.5
1972	4,794	511	10.6
1973	7,162	71	9.0
1974	7,965	663	8.3
1975	7,972	805	10.0
1976	6,000	485	8.0
1977	7,143	825	11.5
1978	7,849	865	11.0
1979	12,096	850	7.0
1980	15,081	1,398	9.2
1981	14,725	1,512	10.2
1982	16,082	1,821	11.3
1983	17,804	2,237	12.5
1984	17,780	2,553	14.3

Archery Hunting — Elk

Date	No. Hunters	Harvest	Percent Success
1968	1,021	35	3.4
1969	934	58	6.2
1970	1,780	29	1.6
1971	2,208	57	2.5
1972	2,966	77	2.5
1973	4,927	112	2.2
1974	5,636	81	1.4
1975	5,344	175	3.2
1976	4,927	198	4.0
1977	6,338	269	4.2
1978	7,238	354	4.8
1979	7,265	363	4.9
1980	9,060	444	4.8
1981	9,263	408	4.4
1982	9,655	504	5.2
1983	9,970	578	5.7
1984	11,053	783	7.0

Archery Hunting — Antelope

Date	No. Hunters	Harvest	Percent Success
1968	106	0	0.0
1969	97	0	0.0
1970	215	34	15.8
1971	235	7	2.9
1972	426	23	5.3
1973	489	22	4.4
1974	489	25	5.1
1975	508	85	16.7
1976	474	60	12.6
1977	498	90	18.0
1978	347	50	14.4
1979	240	7	2.9
1980	366	34	9.2
1981	470	106	2.2
1982	466	57	12.2
1983	631	127	20.1
1984	839	164	19.5

Photo by Frank R. Martin

Appendix A

Sources of Information

STATE OF MONTANA

Montana Department of Fish, Wildlife and Parks
State Headquarters: 1420 E. Sixth Ave., Helena, MT 59620 Phone: 406-444-2535
Regional Offices Region One: 490 North Meridian Rd., Kalispell, MT 59901 Phone: 406-755-5505
Region Two: 3201 Spurgin Rd., Missoula, MT 59801 Phone: 406-721-5808
Region Three: 8695 Huffine Lane, Bozeman, MT 59715 Phone:406-586-5419
Region Four: Route 4041, Box 243, Great Falls, MT 59405 Phone: 406-454-3441
Region Five: 1125 Lake Elmo Dr., Billings, MT 59105 Phone: 406-252-4654
Region Six: Rt. 1, 210, Glasgow, MT 59230 Phone: 406-228-9347
Region Seven: Box 430, Miles City, MT 59301 Phone: 406-232-4365

Travel Promotion Unit, Montana Department of Commerce: 1424 Ninth Ave., Helena, MT 59620 Phone: 406-444-2654. Nonresidents call toll free 1-800-548-3390. An excellent source of general travel information. Be sure to write for their free travel packet on Montana and specifically ask for their *Vacation and Information Guide.* It includes a listing of private and public campgrounds, motels, and other helpful information.

FEDERAL AGENCIES

U.S. Forest Service:

Northern Region Headquarters: U.S. Department of Agriculture, Forest Service, P.O. Box 7669, Federal Building, 200 E. Broadway, Missoula, MT 59807 Phone: 406-329-3711 Contact for general information and advice as to which specific forest you should seek information from. Contact the specific national forest headquarters you plan to visit for maps and information about that forest.

BEAVERHEAD NATIONAL FOREST
Beaverhead National Forest: P.O. Box 1258, 610 N. Montana St., Dillon, MT 59725 Phone: 406-683-2312. Ranger stations at Ennis, Dillon, Sheridan, Wisdom and Wise River.
Dillon Ranger District: 610 N. Montana St., P.O. Box 1258, Dillon, MT 59725 Phone: 406-683-2312.
Madison Ranger District: Route 2, Box 5, Ennis, MT 59729 Phone: 406-682-4253.
Sheridan Ranger District: P.O. Box 428, Sheridan, MT 59749 Phone: 406-842-5432.
Wisdom Ranger District: P.O. Box 238, Wisdom, MT 59761 Phone: 406-689-2431
Wise River Ranger District: P.O. Box 86, Wise River, MT 59762 Phone: 406-839-2201.

BITTERROOT NATIONAL FOREST
Bitterroot National Forest: 316 N. Third St., Hamilton, MT 59840 Phone: 406-363-3131. Ranger stations at Darby, Stevensville and Sula.
Darby Ranger District: Darby, MT 59829 Phone: 406-821-3913.
Stevensville Ranger District: 88 Main St., Stevensville, MT 59870 Phone:

406-777-5461.
   Sula Ranger District: Sula, MT 59871 Phone: 406-821-3201.
   West Fork Ranger District: Darby, MT 59829 Phone: 406-821-3269.

CUSTER NATIONAL FOREST

   Custer National Forest: Also headquarters for all National Grasslands in the Northern Region. P O. Box 2556, 2602 First Ave. N., Billings, MT 59103 Phone: 406-657-6361. Ranger stations at Ashland and Red Lodge.
   Ashland Ranger District: P.O. Box 297, Ashland, MT 59003 Phone: 406-784-2344.
   Beartooth Ranger District: Rt. 2, Box 3420, Red Lodge, MT 59068 Phone: 406-446-2103.

DEER LODGE NATIONAL FOREST

   Deer Lodge National Forest: P.O. Box 400, Federal Building, 400 N. Main St., Butte, MT 59701 Phone: 406-723-6561, ext. 2351. Ranger stations at Butte, Deer Lodge, Philipsburg and Whitehall.
   Butte Ranger District: 2201 White Blvd., Butte, MT 59701 Phone: 406-494-2147.
   Deer Lodge Ranger District: 91 N. Frontage Rd., Deer Lodge, MT 59722 Phone: 406-846-1770.
   Jefferson Ranger District: 405 E. Legion, P.O. Box F, Whitehall, MT 59759 Phone: 406-287-3223.
   Philipsburg Ranger District: P.O. Box H, Philipsburg, MT 59858 Phone: 406-859-3211.

FLATHEAD NATIONAL FOREST

   Flathead National Forest: P.O. Box 147, 1935 Third Ave. E., Kalispell, MT 59901 Phone: 406-755-5401. Ranger stations at Bigfork, Columbia Falls, Hungry Horse and Whitefish.
   Glacier View Ranger District: Columbia Falls, MT 59912 Phone: 406-892-4372.
   Hungry Horse Ranger District: Hungry Horse, MT 59919 Phone: 406-387-5243.
   Spotted Bear Ranger District: Hungry Horse, MT 59919 Phone: Summer, 406-755-7311; Winter, 406-387-5243.
   Swan Lake Ranger District: P.O. Box 370, Bigfork, MT 59911 Phone: 406-837-5081.
   Tally Lake Ranger District: Whitefish, MT 59937 Phone: 406-862-2508.

GALLATIN NATIONAL FOREST

   Gallatin National Forest: P.O. Box 130, 10 East Babcock St., Federal Bldg., Bozeman, MT 59715 Phone: 406-587-5271. Ranger stations at Big Timber, Bozeman, Gardiner, Livingston and West Yellowstone.
   Big Timber Ranger District: P.O. Box A, Big Timber, MT 59011 Phone: 406-932-3647.
   Bozeman Ranger District: 601 Nikles Ave., Box C, Bozeman, MT 59715 Phone: 406-587-5271.
   Gardiner Ranger District: P.O. Box 5, Gardiner, MT 59030 Phone: 406-848-7231.
   Hebgen Lake Ranger District: P.O. Box 520, West Yellowstone, MT 59758 Phone: 406-646-7369.
   Livingston Ranger District: Route 62, Box 3197, Livingston, MT 59047 Phone: 406-222-1892.

HELENA NATIONAL FOREST

   Helena National Forest: 301 S. Park, Room 328, Helena, MT 59626 Phone: 406-449-5201. Ranger stations at Helena, Lincoln and Townsend.
   Helena Ranger District: Federal Bldg., 301 S. Park, P.O. Drawer 10015, Helena, MT 59626 Phone: 406-449-5490.
   Lincoln Ranger District: P.O. Box 234, Lincoln, MT 59639 Phone: 406-362-4265.
   Townsend Ranger District: P.O. Box 29, Townsend, MT 59644 Phone: 406-266-3425.

KOOTENAI NATIONAL FOREST

Kootenai National Forest: Rural Rt. 3, Box 700, Libby, MT. 59923 Phone: 406-293-6211. Ranger stations at Eureka, Fortine, Libby, Rexford, Trout Creek and Troy.

Cabinet Ranger District: Rt. 2, Box 210, Trout Creek, MT 59874 Phone: 406-847-2270.

Fisher River Ranger District: Star Rt. 2, Box 200, Libby, MT 59923 Phone: 406-293-7733.

Fortine Ranger District: P.O. Box 116, Fortine, MT 59918 Phone: 406-882-4451.

Libby Ranger District: Rt. 2, Box 275, Libby, MT 59923   Phone: 406-293-7741.

Rexford Ranger District: P.O. Box 666, Eureka, MT 59917 Phone: 406-296-2536.

Troy Ranger District: P.O. Box E, Troy, MT 59935 Phone: 406-295-4693.

Yaak Ranger District: Rt. 1, Troy, MT 59935 Phone: 406-295-4717.

LEWIS AND CLARK NATIONAL FOREST

Lewis and Clark National Forest: P.O. Box 871, 1601 2nd Ave. N., Federal Bldg., Great Falls, MT 59403 Phone: 406-727-0901. Ranger stations at Choteau, Harlowton, Stanford and White Sulphur Springs. There also are Information Stations at Augusta and Neihart.

Augusta Information Station: P.O. Box 365, Augusta, MT 59410 Phone: 406-562-3247.

Belt Creek Information Station: Neihart, MT 59465 Phone: 406-236-5511.

Judith River Ranger Station: P.O. Box 484, Stanford, MT 59479 Phone: 406-566-2292.

King's Hill Ranger District: P.O. Box A, White Sulphur Springs, MT 59645 Phone: 406-547-3361.

Musselshell Ranger District: P.O. Box F, Harlowton, MT 59036 Phone: 406-632-4391.

Rocky Mountain Ranger District: P.O. Box 340, Choteau, MT 59422 Phone: 406-466-2951.

LOLO NATIONAL FOREST

Lolo National Forest: Fort Missoula, Building 24, Missoula, MT 59801 Phone: 406-329-3557. Ranger stations at Huson, Missoula, Plains, Seeley Lake, Superior and Thompson Falls.

Missoula Ranger District: 5115 Highway 93 S., Missoula, MT 59803 Phone: 406-329-3557.

Ninemile Ranger District: Huson, MT 59846 Phone: 406-626-5201.

Plains Ranger District: Plains, MT 59859 Phone: 406-826-3821.

Seeley Lake Ranger District: P.O. Drawer G, Seeley Lake, MT 59868 Phone: 406-677-2233.

Superior Ranger District: Superior, MT 59872 Phone: 406-822-4233.

Thompson Falls Ranger District: Thompson Falls, MT 59873. Phone: 406-827-3589.

U.S. Bureau of Land Management:

Billings Resource Area Headquarters, 810 E. Main St., Billings, MT 59101 Phone: 406-657-6262

Butte District Office, P.O. Box 3388, Butte, MT 59701 Phone: 406-723-6561

Dillon Resource Area Headquarters, P.O. Box 1048, Dillon, MT 59725 Phone: 406-683-2337

Garnet Resource Area Headquarters, Fort Missoula, P.O. Box 4427, Missoula, MT 59801 Phone: 406-329-3914

Bureau of Land Management: Highway 2 W., Glasgow, MT 59230 Phone: 406-265-5891.

Havre Resource Area Headquarters, P.O. Building-Drawer 911, Havre, MT 59501 Phone: 406-265-5891

Lewistown District Office, Airport Road, Drawer 1160, Lewistown, MT 59457 Phone: 406-538-7461

Miles City District Office, P.O. Box 940, Miles City, MT 59301 Phone: 406-232-4331N   **Phillips Resource Area Headquarters**, 501 South 2nd Street E., P.O. Box B, Malta, MT 59538 Phone: 406-654-1240

U.S. Fish and Wildlife Service:

For information from the national wildlife refuges located in Montana, write or call the Refuge Manager at each site.

Benton Lake National Wildlife Refuge, P.O. Box 450, Black Eagle, MT 59414 Phone: 406-727-7400

Bowdoin National Wildlife Refuge, P.O. Box J, Malta, MT 59538

Charles M. Russell National Wildlife Refuge, Box 110, Lewistown, MT 59457 Phone: 406-538-8706

Medicine Lake National Wildlife Refuge, Medicine Lake, MT 59247 Phone: 406-789-2305

Lee Metcalf National Wildlife Refuge, Box 257, Stevensville, MT 59870 Phone: 406-777-5552

National Bison Range, Moiese, MT 59824 Phone: 406-644-2354

Ninepipe and Pablo National Wildlife Refuge, Moiese, MT 59824 Phone: 406-644-2354

Red Rock Lakes National Wildlife Refuge: Monida Star Rt., Box 15, Lima, MT 59739 Phone: 406-276-3347.

U.S. Geological Survey:

U.S. Geological Survey, Distribution Section, Federal Center, Building 41, Denver, CO 80225. The best source of maps.

OUTFITTERS

Montana Outfitters and Guides Association, Box 631, Hot Springs, MT 59845. They'll send you a copy of their booklet listing accredited association members.

For a complete listing of licensed outfitters in Montana, write Supervisor of Outfitters, Montana Department of Fish, Wildlife and Parks, 1420 E. Sixth Ave., Helena, MT 59620.

Appendix B

Bibliography — Additional Information Sources

Bugling for Elk, A Complete Guide to Early-Season Elk Hunting, By Dwight Schuh, Stoneydale Press Publishing Co., StevE)70, 1983.

Elk Hunting in the Northern Rockies, By Ed Wolff, Stoneydale Press Publishing Co., Stevensville, MT 59870, 1984.

Game Management in Montana, Edited by Thomas W. Mussehl and F. W. Howell, Montana Department of Fish, Wildlife and Parks, Helena, MT 59601 1971.

History of Fisheries Management in Montana, By William Alvord, Montana Department of Fish, Wildlife and Parks, unpublished, 1975.

Hunting Upland Birds, Charles F. Waterman, Stoeger Publishing Co., Hackensack, N.J., 1972.

Hunting Rutting Whitetails, By Gene Wensel, Hamilton, MT 59840. An excellent, insightful book by one of the country's best bowhunters.

Montana Big Game Trophies, By Kenneth Greer, Montana Department of Fish, Wildlife and Parks, various editions.

Montana's Bob Marshall Country, By Rich Graetz, Montana Magazine, Helena, MT 59601, 1985.

Montana Hunting, 1980 Edition, By Dale A. Burk, Stoneydale Press Publishing Co., Stevensville, MT 59870, 1980.

Montana Hunting, 1981 Edition, By Dale A. Burk, Stoneydale Press Publishing Co., Stevensville, MT 59870, 1981.

Montana Outdoors Magazine, various issues, published by Montana Department of Fish, Wildlife and Parks, Helena, MT 59621.

Montana Wildlife, By Robert C. Gildart with Jan Wassink, Montana Magazine Inc., Helena, MT 59601, 1982.

Outdoorsman's Emergency Manual, By Anthony J. Accerano, Winchester Press, New York, N.Y., 1973.

The Outdoor Observer, Charles Elliott, Outdoor Life-E.P. Dutton & Co., New York, N.Y., 1969. One of the best written and most interesting books on the outdoors I've ever read.

Packing in on Mules and Horses, By Smoke Elser and Bob Brown, Mountain Press Publishing Co., Missoula, MT 59801, 1982.

Statutes, State of Montana, A Compilation of Statutes Relating to Fish, Wildlife and Parks, Outdoor Recreation and Certain Other Natural Resources in the State of Montana, James W. Flynn, Director, Montana Department of Fish, Wildlife and Parks, Helena, MT 59601, 1983.

MAP SOURCES

U.S. Forest Service: Individual forest maps showing the location of developed camp and picnic areas are available from the forest supervisor offices for a small fee. If maps of more than one forest are desired, you may order them from the Regional Fiscal Agent, Box 7129, Missoula, MT 59807. Very useful topographical maps of each forest are available for a fee upon writing the specific forests or stopping by the various ranger stations or supervisors' offices. Also, each ranger district has a Recreation Opportunity Guide of inventoried recreation opportunities available. These are available for viewing at district ranger offices.

Appendix C

Chronology of Wildlife History — Montana

1805-06 — Lewis and Clark Expedition travels through Montana, first recorded details of wildlife and the hunting of them.

1855 — Sir George Gore, the European "gentleman hunter" hunted in Montana with his retinue of 41 men on the first recorded outfitted hunt in the state.

1806-1850 — Fur trade in full glory period with beaver pelts the main prize. Little impact on Montana's wildlife other than beaver as the trappers killed only enough game to satisfy their needs.

1850-1900 — Booming trade in elk, deer and buffalo hides. Permanent impact on Montana's wildlife populations.

1860s — Discovery and development of gold camps in Montana, arrival of the river steamers on the upper Missouri. Arrival of trail herds of cattle.

1860s-1883 — Headlong slaughter of buffalo occurs.

1869 — First laws protecting game birds, quail and partridge protected by closed season for three years.

1872 — First closed season on buffalo, moose, elk, deer, bighorn sheep, mountain goats, antelope and hares, Feb. 1 to Aug. 15 each year.

1873-74 — Passenger pigeon extinct.

1876 — Battle of the Little Bighorn. Led directly to opening of eastern plains to cattle grazing, led to changes in rangeland vegetation and contributed to decline of big game populations.

— First closed season on furbearing animals, closed April 1 to Oct. 1 each year on beaver, otter, marten fishers.

— First closed season on ducks and geese from May 15 to Aug. 10 each year.

1877 — Act passed making it unlawful to kill game animals for hides alone without using or selling meat.

— Trapping of beaver prohibited except on private lands.

— Unlawful to hunt or chase game animals with dogs.

— Sale of game birds for market purposes prohibited.

1883 — Act prohibiting destroying nests of game birds and waterfowl, or to take eggs away from nests.

1893 — First year-around closed season on moose and elk.

1895 — First Fish and Game Board authorized by Legislature.

— Big game season set by Legislature: Sept. 1-Jan. 1. Limits: 8 deer, 8 bighorn sheep, 8 mountain goats, 8 antelope, 2 moose, 2 elk.

1897 — First daily bag limit placed on game birds. No person may kill more than 20 grouse or prairie chickens in one day.

1901 — W. F. Scott, first state Fish and Game Warden (Director) appointed by governor.

— Bobwhite introduced near Kalispell, Flathead County.

— First license required (nonresidents only) to take game animals and game birds. Nonresidents required to purchase hunting license of $25 for game animals, $15 for game birds.

1902 — First Biennial Report of State Fish and Game Warden W. F. Scott. The official documentation of the wildlife situation in Montana was underway.

1903 — Bobwhite introduced in Utica, Judith Basin County, and Fergus County.

— Taxidermist license required.

— Guides license required.

1905 — First resident hunting and fishing licenses required at a cost of $1.00. One license per family required.

1908 — First Montana area set aside for big game use by U.S. Forest Service in Upper Gallatin.

1909 — First daily bag limit on wild ducks set at 20 per day.

1910 — Statewide season open Oct. 1-Dec. 1 for 3 deer, 1 elk, 1 sheep, 1 goat (closed on antelope,. moose, caribou, bison).

1911 — First game preserves created by Legislature primarily for antelope but also for deer and game birds: Snow Creek Game Preserve, Dawson County, Pryor Mountain Game Preserve and Gallatin Preserve.

1912 — Bobwhite introduced in Deer Lodge Valley, Deer Lodge and Powell Counties.

1913 — Montana Fish and Game Commission organized.

— Sun River Game Preserve created by Legislature.

1915 — Bobwhite introduced on Wildhorse Island on Flathead Lake, Lake County.

— Hungarian partridge found near Plains, Sanders County (specimen found dead and identified).

— Season closed on bighorn sheep and remained closed until 1953.

1916 — Last Audubon sheep killed in Garfield County.

— Closed season on moose, bison, caribou, antelope, beaver, bighorn sheep, mountain goat, quail, Chinese pheasant and Hungarian partridge.

— Open big game season Oct. 1-Dec. 15. Limit: Two deer per season, any age or sex; one elk per season (only in certain counties). — Open game bird season Sept. 1-Oct. 1. Limit: Five birds per person per day, grouse, prairie chickens, foolhens, sage hens, pheasants or partridge in southeastern Montana. Game bird season Sept. 15-Oct. 15 all other counties not mentioned above.

1917 — Deer bag limit changed from two deer to one deer statewide.

— First counties closed to deer hunting in Yellowstone, Rosebud, Custer, Dawson and Richland.

— Nonresident license raised to $15.00 from $10.00.

— Prairie chicken taken (only recorded specimen in 1921) Huntley, Yellowstone County.

— First bird preserve, Flathead Lake Bird Preserve (two islands), Flathead County.

— Resident hunting and fishing license raised from $1 to $1.50.

1917-18 — Gambel quail (31 dozen) planted in Teton, Missoula, Musselshell, Yellowstone, Sanders, Broadwater, Gallatin, Park, Choteau, Dawson, Carbon, Custer Counties.

— Ringnecked pheasant planted in Flathead and Lincoln Counties from stock in Utah.

1918 — Migratory Bird Treaty between Great Britain (Canada) and the United States signed providing national authority to manage migratory game birds and protecting many nongame bird species.

1919 — Closed season on deer in Valley, Roosevelt, Sheridan, Yellowstone, Rosebud, Custer, Richland and Dawson Counties.

— Restriction on use of automobiles to kill game.

— First license required for taking fur animals. Marten license fee $1.

1920 — Nonresident general (hunting and fishing) license raised to $50 from $15.

— Commission purchased 150 pair of pheasants from Oregon.

1921 — Commission given authority to establish game preserves. Twelve state game preserves and refuges had been established in Montana.

— Present five-member Fish and Game Commission system appointed by the governor as provided by law. Granted power to allot Fish and Game districts and to close or open seasons under certain conditions.

— Resident hunting and fishing license fee raised from $1.50 top $2.

— Nonresident hunting and fishing license fee changed from $50 to $30 and remained $30 until 1947.

— Deer seasons set for Nov. 1-Dec. 1, limited to one buck and closed in Yellowstone, Rosebud, Custer, Powder River, Carter, Richland, Roosevelt, McCone, Dawson, Stillwater, Gallatin, Teton, Phillips, Garfield, Valley Counties and a portion of Fergus County.

1922 — Commission released 1,500 pheasants in state.

— First commission-created game preserve established in Tobacco Root Mountains, Madison County.

1922-26 — Hungarian partridge purchased in Europe and released in all counties of the state by Fish and Game Commission (1,000 in 1922, 2,000 in 1923, 2,000 in 1925, 1,000 in 1926).

1925 — Muskrat farm established at Swan Lake, Lake County (five fenced areas, billed at "Largest in America").

— 3,027 antelope for Montana in 44 areas by Biological Survey in U.S. Agriculture Department Bulletin.

1926 — First land acquired for game management purposes (27 acres at Red Rock Lakes), Beaverhead County.

1928 — First pheasant season in Montana.

1929 — 17 Legislature-created preserves. — First Hungarian partridge season in Montana.

— First game farm at Warm Springs.

— First goat season in West Bitterroot, Ravalli County, since 1914.

1930 — 33 game preserves totaling 2,000,000 acres.

1931 — First big game resident license to take deer and elk, $1.

— Fur dealer's license required, fee $1.

1932 — California quail released in Deer Lodge County from game farm.

1933 — First chukars released in Montana, Dawson County.

1934 — First duck hunting stamps sold in Montana.,

1935 — Game farm established at Billings.

— First permit antelope season in all of Carter and Powder River Counties except game preserve.

— 46 state game preserves in Montana (the maximum number of game preserves in effect at one time).

1935-36 — Valley quail (218) liberated in Yellowstone, Lake, Big Horn, Granite and Lewis and Clark Counties.

1936 — Antelope season in Chouteau County, 400 permits.

— Three preserves abandoned (Albert Wood, Carbon County, Spotted Bear).

— Statewide buck law declared.

— 29,699 resident big game licenses sold at $1 each.

— Game bird seasons closed statewide due to severe drought except for four-day mountain grouse season in Lincoln County.

— Eight chukars released in Stillwater County.

— First winter deer ranges leased in Sanders, Missoula and Powell Counties.

— C. M. Russell Game Ranch (Fort Peck Game Range) created by Congress (97,000 acres).

1937 — First chukar eggs from Oregon to Warm Springs State Game Farm.

1938-42 — Ten plants of chukars in eastern Montana with an average of 23 birds for each plant (eggs from Washington, Wyoming, California).

1939 — State versus Rathbone case which established important precedent to game damage problems.

1940 — First acquisition of the Judith River Game Range for elk winter range, Judith Basin County.

— First big game manager position created in Fish and Game Department.

1941 — The Federal Aid in Wildlife Restoration Program (the Pittman-Robertson Program) began. Big game and game bird surveys were initiated.

— Fish and Game Commission given regulatory power over opening and closing seasons, setting of bag limits and creating game preserves.

— Commission policy established setting up an investigational program to obtain scientific data as a basis for wildlife management.

— First goats transplanted in Montana from Deep Creek, Teton County, to Crazy Mountains, Sweetgrass County.

— First large-scale program of live trapping and transplanting of beaver undertaken by the department with 1,986 animals transplanted.

— First four-day special season on either-sex deer exclusive of fawns in portion of Madison County.

1942 — First bighorn sheep transplanted from Sun River, Teton County, to Gates of the Mountains, Lewis and Clark County.

— Surveys estimate 14,000 antelope in eastern and central Montana.

— First hen pheasant season in Montana (Yellowstone County).

— First one-month, either-sex deer season in portion of Madison County.

1943 — First mule deer transplanted from National Bison Range, Lake County, to Glendive badlands, Dawson County.

— Antelope hunting renewed in Montana on an annual basis (750 permits).

— First extended special either-sex season on deer, Nov. 15-Dec. 31 or until 500 head taken in portion of Madison County.

— First one-month special either-sex deer season in portion of Ravalli County.

1945 — First whitetailed deer transplanted from Bowser Lake, Flathead County, to East Rosebud, Stillwater or Carbon County.

— First moose seasons in portions of Park, Gallatin, Madison and Beaverhead Counties.

1946 — First antelope transplanted in Montana from Winston area, Broadwater County, to Horseshoe Hills, Gallatin County.

1947 — Beaver transplanting program discontinued except for beaver causing damage.

— resident big game license fee changed from $1 to $2.

— The bounty on coyotes discontinued.

— First special closed season on one species of deer (whitetail deer, Broadwater County).

1948 — Blackfoot-Clearwater Game Range in Missoula and Powell Counties and Sun River Game Range in Lewis and Clark Counties were acquired.

— Bighorn sheep from Colorado were released in special holding pasture in Garfield County.

1949 — Valley quail (12 pairs) obtained from Oregon were introduced in Lake County.

— Forage surveys on state game ranges started.

— Milk River waterfowl habitat acquired in Phillips County.

1950 — First statewide mountain goat and bighorn sheep studies completed.

— A study of pheasant stocking in the Gallatin Valley indicated the high cost and biological limitations of planting birds.

1951 — Either-sex deer season, three days in northwestern Montana. The remainder of the state was bucks only or closed.

— Heavy chukar planting began in Montana (continued until 1956 when Commission discontinued raising and releasing chukars).

— Gallatin Game Range acquired to provide elk winter range.

1952 — Either-sex deer season of two weeks in western Montana, three days in southwestern and southcentral Montana. Bucks only or closed elsewhere.

— First Department studies on effects of insecticides on bird life completed in eastern Montana.

— Fox Lake Waterfowl Area acquired in Richland County.

1953 — Bighorn sheep hunting began with a limited permit system.

— Mountain goat hunting changed to limited permit system.

— Freezeout Lake waterfowl hunting area acquired in Teton County.

— Flathead Lake goose nesting area acquired.

— First bow-and-arrow hunting licenses issued.

— Ninepipe waterfowl and small game management area started, Lake County, as the first in a series of acquisitions.

1954 — First turkey plant in Judith Mountains, Fergus County, with 13 birds from Colorado.

— Madison-Bear Creek and Bull Mountain elk winter range acquired in Madison County.

— Bowser lake deer range acquired in Flathead County.

— A full-time wildlife extension program was started at the University of Montana in Missoula to serve western Montana. A similar program followed at Montana State College in Bozeman for eastern Montana.

1955 — Second turkey plant (18 Merriam turkeys from Wyoming) to Long Pines, Carter County.

— One-month either-sex deer season in approximately half the state.

— Resident big game license fees changed from $2 to $3.

— District organization and district approach to game management by the Montana Department of Fish and Game began.

— First $20 nonresident deer and antelope licenses.

— Estimated statewide deer harvest reaches 100,000.

— A comprehensive big game management policy was adopted by the Fish and Game Commission.

1956 — First general two-deer, either-sex season in northwest, southwest and southcentral Montana to occur since 1917.

— Big game salting program abandoned except for trapping and research purposes.

— First deer archery season statewide.

— Otter taken off the protected list.

— Chukar game farm at Moiese closed and further attempts to establish this species throughout the state abandoned.

— One month either-sex deer season except for northcentral and northeast Montana.

— The Montana Fish and Game Commission adopted a policy of opening a big game season on Oct. 15 or the first Sunday after Oct. 15.

1957 — Deer and elk hunting units established in each Fish and Game administrative district.

— Deer harvest of 134,000, which included 90,000 bucks or more than twice the number of bucks killed under the last statewide bucks-only season.

— Haymaker elk winter range acquired on south side of Little Belt Mountains, Wheatland County.

1958 — First Merriam turkey hunt in Long Pines, Carter County.

— First statewide bird harvest estimate.

— First statewide either-sex deer seasons.

— The bounty on bobcats was discontinued.

— Blue grouse banding indicated that more liberal hunting seasons could be allowed.

1959 — Upland game bird seasons increased in length and the daily total limit of three birds increased to provide limits ranging from three to five birds per species.

— Pheasant season with hen in bag in Teton County on an experimental basis.

— First special turkey license issued.

— Antelope, moose, sheep and goat special season units were organized into administrative districts.

— First use of automatic data processing by the Fish and Game Department to obtain game harvest information from hunter questionnaires.

— Thirty-six fisher were introduced into three areas of northwestern Montana.

— The Fish and Game Commission adopted a policy which specified that the western Merriam turkey would be the only turkey planted in Montana.

1960 — Mountain grouse seasons increased to 57 days.

— Bitterroot and Madison-Wall Creek elk winter ranges acquired in Ravalli and Madison

Counties.
1961 — Montana west of the Continental Divide placed in the Pacific Flyway.
— First either-sex pheasant season in Montana.
1962 — Cooperative Gallatin elk management plan initiated with Fish and Game Department, U.S. Forest Service and U.S. Park Service.
— Fleecer Mountain Game range acquired primarily for elk winter range in Silver Bow County.
— Bounty on mountain lion discontinued.
1963 — First spring season on turkey gobblers in Long Pines area.
— Forest grouse-DDT studies undertaken during spruce budworm spraying on Bitterroot National Forest. Nearly 3 million acres sprayed in Montana in past decade.
— Statewide mountain goat harvest over 500, compared to 30 to 130 per year from 1941 to 1945.
1964 — Tenth consecutive year that statewide deer harvest exceeded 100,000, and ninth consecutive year that hunter success exceeded 90 percent.
— Big game license forms changed, enabling hunters to purchase deer tags and/or elk tags separately.
— DDT contaminations in wildlife led to Fish and Game Commission policy statement protesting further use of chlorinated hydrocarbon insecticides on public lands and urging research on effects of herbicides on habitat. (DDT was not used for spruce budworm control after 1963.)
— A banner year for bird hunters. Over 370,000 prairie and mountain grouse harvested, compared to 130,000 in 1958. A record number, 164,000, of hungarian partridge were harvested. Pheasant harvest exceeded 350,000.
1965 — Beginning of 10-year cooperative Fish and Game-Bureau of Land Management-Montana State University research project to determine the ecological effects of spraying sagebrush.
— Beginning of $35 black bear licenses.
— Pacific Flyway boundary moved eastward from Continental Divide.
— Pablo waterfowl hunting area acquired in Lake County.
1966 — First special teal season in Central Flyway portion of Montana.
— Study of Merriam turkey ecology published which has provided guidelines for transplanting new areas and allowing more liberal hunting of established flocks.
1967 — The game license system was modified and fees were generally increased. A new Sportsman's License and a youth license were established by law.
— The first grizzly bear license and grizzly trophy license were issued.
— Contract research with the U.S. Fish and Wildlife Service evaluating experimental forest-insecticides used to replace DDT was completed on the Bitterroot National Forest.
— Three-mile Game Range acquired for elk winter range in Ravalli County.
— Eighth consecutive year that statewide forest grouse harvest exceeded 120,000, compared to 72,500 in 1958. Estimated forest grouse harvest exceeds that of pheasants, which was 97,108.
— Tenth year of turkey hunting in Montana with nearly 5,000 harvested since the first 18 were planted in 1955.
1968 — Canyon Ferry Game Management area project for waterfowl habitat development and public hunting was initiated.
— A special post-season hunt on mallard drakes was held in the Central Flyway portion of Montana.
— Statewide elk harvest estimated at 16,000, equaling the previous peak harvest in 1955.
1969 — The license system was changed to issue Conservation Licenses and stamps for birds. Big game combination licenses were discontinued.
— A pheasant hen was allowed in statewide bag limits.
— Twelfth consecutive year that statewide moose harvests exceeded 400, with hunter

success usually between 70 to 80 percent.

— Investigations of mercury contamination of game birds frequenting grain-growing areas were initiated.

— Isaac Homestead small game management area acquired in Treasure County.

— Deer hunter success 80 percent. Success exceeded 80 percent in 13 of past 15 years and is double that before 1952.

1970 — The first swan season (500 permits) at the Freezout Lake area.

— The Beartooth Game Range providing key elk winter range and other wildlife habitat was acquired.

1973 — Blacktail Wildlife Management Area acquired.

1974 — Hen pheasants removed from game bag.

— Extensive winter kill of Yellowstone Elk and South Gallatin and Yellowstone (Gardiner) areas.

1975 — Permit required for taking either-sex deer began to appear in hunting regulations.

1976 — Ear Mountain Wildlife Managemnt Area acquired.

— Mt. Haggin Wildlife Management Area acquired.

1979 — Blackleaf Wildlife Management Area acquired.

1981 — Big Lake Wildlife Management Area acquired.

— Rest-rotation grazing implemented on Mt. Haggin.

1984 — Dove season established.

1985 — Buffalo season established under carefully controlled and restrictive regulations.

— Record sellout of 17,000 nonresident hunting license occurs; all taken in five and a half days.

Appendix D

Sportsman-Conservation Groups

I strongly recommend membership in local, state and national conservation organizations concerning hunting, not only for educational purposes but also to lend your assistance to the cause of sound, scientific wildlife management and the practice and promulgation of hunter ethics. Listed below are the names and addresses of several Montana-based organizations.

Statewide Groups

Montana Bowhunters' Association
P.O. Box 551
Ashland, MT 59003

Montana Wildlife Federation
P.O. Box 3526
Bozeman, MT 59715

Montana Wilderness Association
P.O. Box 635
Helena, MT 59624

Rocky Mountain Elk Foundation
Route 3, Wilderness Plateau
Troy, Montana 59935
Note: A national group headquartered in Montana. Highly recommended to those who wish to promote long-term perspective of elk management and elk hunting.

Local Groups

This represents a partial listing of sportsman's and hunting groups in Montana.

Anaconda Sportsmen's Group
No. 2 Cherry St.
Anaconda, MT 59711

Custer Rod and Gun Club
2804 Pleasant St.
Miles City, MT 59301

Flathead Wildlife Association
254 Fairfield Dr.
Kalispell, MT 59901

Gallatin Wildlife Association
317 S. 6th Ave.
Bozeman, MT 59715

Hill County Wildlife Association
Box 282
Havre, MT 59501

Lewistown Rod and Gun Club
116 Hilger Ave.
Lewistown, MT 59457

Libby Rod and Gun Club
Libby, MT 59923

Mineral County Sportsman's Group
P.O. Box 361
Superior, MT 59872

Polson Outdoors
Polson, MT 59860

Prickly Pear Sportsman's Association
5735 Kerr Dr.
Helena, MT 59601

Ravalli County Fish and Wildlife Association
P.O. Box 653
Hamilton, MT 59840

Skyline Sportsmen
Box 2
Ramsey, MT 59748

Teton County Sportsmen's Association
RR 2, Box 116
Choteau, MT 59422

Western Montana Fish and Game Association
23945 Bonita
Ranger Station
Clinton, MT 59825

Billings Rod and Gun Club
2114 Constellation Tr.
Billings, MT 59105

Lower Yellowstone Outdoors
808 N. Meade
Glendive, MT 59301